BARON AT THE BALLET

BARON
AT
THE BALLET

Introduction and Commentary
by
ARNOLD L. HASKELL

Foreword by
SACHEVERELL SITWELL

COLLINS
ST JAMES'S PLACE, LONDON
1950

PRINTED IN GREAT BRITAIN
TEXT PRINTED AND THE BOOK BOUND BY
WILLIAM COLLINS SONS AND CO. LTD., GLASGOW
MONOCHROME AND COLOUR PHOTOGRAVURE SECTIONS PRINTED BY
HARRISON AND SONS LTD., HIGH WYCOMBE, BUCKS

To
MY MOTHER
who bought me my first
camera

FOREWORD
by Sacheverell Sitwell

I CANNOT be alone in wishing I were a painter whenever I see a good dancer. There must be many more in the audience who agree with me. And yet, how few such painters there have been ! The famous portrait of Camargo tells us little or nothing we did not know before. I prefer to imagine that great dancer for myself; and I dare say my imagination is nearer the truth. Fragonard's Mlle. Guimard—and surely Fragonard loved to watch dancing!—is no better. I can recollect plenty of photographs, but no good portrait of Karsavina. I can think of no worthy painting of Margot Fonteyn, the prima ballerina assoluta of our time. But I can remember a lovely pastel portrait of Barberina, a Venetian dancer, by Rosalba, that used to be in the picture gallery at Dresden, in the same room as La Belle Chocolatière by Liotard. And what a lovely portrait it was! A vision from the Venetian Carnival, but only the head and shoulders of Barberina; enough to set one thinking, but only of Barberina in private life, off the stage, perhaps shopping in the Merceria or eating ices at Florian's. But nothing, nothing of Barberina dancing; who assuredly was a beautiful dancer and, I think, one of the stars of Ludwigsburg, where the Duke of Wurtemberg, a pluralist, if ever there was one, had three theatres of his own, one French and two Italian, twenty principal dancers and one hundred in the corps de ballet—and Noverre for choreographer! You can read about it in Casanova's *Memoirs*. No. Watteau is the painter of all painters who should have *drawn* the ballet, and I write that contradiction on purpose, because Watteau was the most exquisite draughtsman of persons there has ever been. Can I not imagine his red chalk drawings of Moira Shearer as Cinderella, *en sanguine*? But it does not seem to have been even within the genius of Watteau to paint or draw figures in motion. One painter, and one painter only, Degas, has achieved that. But Degas, unfortunately, did not live in a great era for the ballet; his long life filled the interval between the age of the Romantic Ballet and our own. Even so, he has left superb paintings of dancers at practice and in action. But his acidulous mind would hardly admit of physical beauty in a dancer. We must not look for that in his paintings, any more than for refinement in his seamstresses, or breeding in his racehorses. But of one

7

thing we may feel certain : Degas would have delighted in the modern action photographs of dancers. For they have flashes of instantaneous observation ; they report truths of movement, and a poetry of movement, that the human eye, unassisted, cannot grasp and hold.

When I was young there was only one company of dancers, the Russian Ballet. There were dancers, of course, at the Paris Opéra and at the Scala, but no one was interested. Now there are half a dozen companies, at least, with first-rate dancers, even if the ballets they produce are not all works of art. The number of dancers, owing to improved methods of teaching, is ten times what it was, and I suppose the audience is fifty or a hundred times bigger than it used to be. Some of the best dancers in the world are English; and so are one or two of the choreographers. The Sadler's Wells Ballet alone must have given pleasure to a million or more people since that opening night at Covent Garden in February, 1946. And luckily none of this need now be forgotten. The camera, in clever hands, remembers and perpetuates it all, good and bad. But let no one think it is easy to take ballet photographs! Baron has shown me early photographs that he took of dancers, and looking at them you could see his advancement in his art· The camera is a machine; but it has to be controlled by taste and intelligence. Not even the most consummate actors or dancers " take " of themselves. It is the " touch " of an intelligence, and not an accident, that makes a good photograph. The old master among photographers of dancers is Baron de Meyer. Some of his photographs of Nijinsky in *Spectre de la Rose*, in *L'Après-Midi*, in *Pavillon d'Armide*, are perfect works of art and the only memorials of that dancer. But I believe that only one of these, from *Pavillon d'Armide*, is in action. The rest are studio portraits. In this present collection there are action studies in plenty and nearly every prominent dancer of our day is represented. To lovers of the ballet like myself, and how many others, part of the poetry of dancing is in reckoning of the hours of work and years of training that make the life of a dancer. I know of no other profession that works so hard. It is nearer to a religion than any other career that I know, and almost as serious. And it interferes, nearly always, with their meals! It is of the difficulties of that long training that we must think when judging, for instance, one " Giselle " against another. Baron's photographs will be valued when the company of dancers, here assembled in black and white and colour, is long past its prime.

SACHEVERELL SITWELL

CONTENTS

COLOUR PLATES

PREFACE
by Baron

IT WAS in 1938 that I first conceived the idea of doing a book of ballet photographs! I had quite enough material—more than most photographers even in those early days. I had been at it for some three years, hard at it, and dead broke doing it. By 1939 I was on the point of sorting out the pictures and a publisher —by 1940 I was on my flat feet, up and down the barrack square as a 2nd Lieutenant in the P.B.I.

After the war, there was a ballet boom and a spate of books appeared written by almost anyone who could think of some excuse to go to press. This, however, is my first effort—the fruits of ten years (leaving out the war period) of ballet photography. It has been quite a labour to do it and I hope it will have been worth while.

The easiest way to start to take ballet pictures is to do so from the stalls, but it isn't the best way. To the man behind the camera, creative photography is as exciting as any artistic achievement. I can remember many moments of genuine ecstasy when taking pictures of ballet, more than in any other branch of work which I have undertaken. I have spent countless hours standing in stalls and balconies, or in the wings, taking action pictures—and many more watching and designing my own photographic compositions. On the whole, action shots taken during a performance do not satisfy one's creative instincts. It is rare to get a completely satisfying shot, particularly in theatre lighting which is insufficient to get really perfect technical quality except in abnormal lighting conditions.

So the great majority of photographs you will see in this book are taken either in my studio, or *on* the stage during a special photocall, which I was fortunate enough to be asked to do. Many you will see are action pictures, but they have been lit and posed especially for the camera, and thus a greater technical excellence is possible, and a chance to arrange composition, pose and lighting. For this type of picture I would refer particularly to those of *Giselle* on pages 28-31, which are all played solely for the camera. This also applies to all the American section, except the dance of Hagar in *Pillar of Fire*. This pas de deux is technically poor, but both Arnold Haskell and myself think they give a true atmosphere to this most beautifully created passage—one of the most moving in modern ballet.

I referred just now to the thrill one gets sometimes out of making ballet pictures. I have had many such thrilling moments. To me among the most satisfying posed action shots are those on pages 34 (*Giselle*—Toumanova, lower), 48 (Babilée), 75 (*Adam Zero*), 83 (Fonteyn), 93 (Shearer), 97 (May), 111 (Helpmann), 135 (*Jardin aux Lilas*), 141 (*Romeo and Juliet*), 152 (Babilée), 171 (Jeanmaire), 179 (Massine), 190 (Skibine), 201 (*Carmen*), 209 (*Carmen*).

Many of these pictures have an element of luck in their success—action photography is, like bridge, a percentage game: you can reduce the element of luck through skill and experience. One of the roughest jobs in composing a book of this description is the final selection of material—it has been a monumental and at times aggravating problem to know what to leave out and what to include. Thank Heaven that Haskell, with his vast store of knowledge, chronological mind and unfailing good taste, was able to edit this work, at least to my entire satisfaction. My sincere thanks are due to him for his patience when constant inspection of the same photographs might have led to nausea or at least to pictorial indigestion.

I wish to acknowledge my gratitude to my colleague Reginald Eyre, who worked with me on many of the photocalls, particularly before the war; to Sacheverell Sitwell who, as ballet-goer, eminent writer, and friend, has been kind enough to write the Foreword; to my colleague, Eugène Rubin who composed the montage on pages 213-15, to the management of Sadler's Wells and other companies who have never refused co-operation; and lastly, to the dancers themselves who, after all, make this book.

BARON

THE BALLET SCENE TODAY
A Survey

INTRODUCTION

As a photographer Baron is inevitably interested above all things in the looks and personality of the dancer. The eternal sylphide, however beautiful an etching in black and white, soon begins to pall as an abstract image, but to fix for all time a Fonteyn or a Chauviré as a sylphide gives the photographer immense satisfaction. He has secured a precious and enduring record. Even if at times it is only a sentimental record, that too is of value in an art of tradition. Would that we could see a photograph of Gautier's divine Carlotta, for him the only Giselle; catch a glimpse of La Sylphide; of her pagan rival, the handsome Spaniard of the North; or better still, have fixed for ever a moment of the *Pas de Quatre*. The young dancers of to-day can at any rate have some idea of how Pavlova, Nijinsky or Karsavina appeared at the height of their fame.

In this volume Baron deals with their successors and covers a vast territory, practically the whole period of the greatest popularity of the art since the Romantic period, the period of the democratisation of ballet.

The camera cannot, however, tell the whole story, and in the general introduction to the various sections, and in the captions, I intend to give some commentary. It must necessarily be subjective, if it is not to degenerate into a series of complimentary write-ups in which every ballet is a masterpiece and every dancer charming and graceful. (Incidentally " charming and graceful " in critical jargon are equivalent to the " satisfactory " of the school report, whilst " interesting " means that the critic has been struck dumb by the enormity of the performance.)

The opinions do not commit Baron any more than the choice of photographs commits the writer. Each one has been left at perfect liberty.

THE DIAGHILEFF HEIRS

In the last section I used the words, " the period of the democratisation of ballet."

That is the keynote to all that has happened since the death of the giant Serge Diaghileff in 1929. During his lifetime ballet and Diaghileff were synonymous.

The great Diaghileff dancers even up to the period of Danilova, his last ballerina, were products of a school paid for out of the Russian Emperor's privy purse. They received an education without haste or stint, their futures were assured. While nominally the Diaghileff Ballet was a commercial undertaking, unlike the Imperial Theatres at home, in fact it depended entirely upon the support of wealthy and discerning patrons starting with the Grand Duke Vladimir and ending with Madame Chanel. It would be inaccurate to say that Diaghileff never knew financial straits—there was the disaster of 1921—but for the larger part of his career he could please himself and himself alone, indulging his taste of the moment, as if he had been the director of a private company. Follow the chronological development of his ballet, it is an important chapter in the history of European art, and you will be following the artistic development of a man through Russian neo-romanticism to the *avant garde* art of Paris. What Diaghileff felt and thought at any given period from 1909 to 1929 was transferred to the stage. His audience was composed of the large family of those good Europeans who to-day have almost disappeared through the politics and economics of this new dark age—the age of the good housewife and the little man, who do not know much about art but who know what they like. Had Diaghileff thought in terms of box office he would have gone on an endless tour with *Les Sylphides*, *Schéhérazade* and *The Polovtsian Dances* from *Prince Igor*. The formula would have paid handsome dividends. In that case he would also have had to listen to the public or, worse still, to the booking-agents who always aim below the public taste, in the casting of his ballets, thereby working his dancers to death through boredom as well as through the wear and tear of cabin-trunk existence.

With Diaghileff there died a whole conception of ballet. Also, his death came at a time when the conception itself might for economic reasons have become impossible. Personally I believe that this extraordinary man would have met and triumphed over the new conditions, but the question does not arise.

His death released those artists who were to create the new Ballet which this volume records. While he lived there was one ballet—I am not forgetting the Paris Opéra and the Russian theatres—a few years after there were many, all of them fighting over the inheritance, an inheritance that had been dissipated and split into fragments. The public increased in numbers but decreased in knowledge and discernment. They were becoming " fans," autograph hunters, clutterers-up of stage doors, users of artists' christian names and such-like.

The heirs had one thing in common: the necessity of filling the house throughout the year, consequently the necessity of providing popular works. To do this the whole orientation had to be altered. With Diaghileff ballet as a whole mattered, and the whole meant the expression of an idea by composers, painters, choreographers and dancers. With the heirs the accent was always on the dancers. As

America was their main stamping ground; they borrowed the notion of stars from the films. In the Diaghileff Ballet such dancers as Danilova, Doubrovska, Tchernicheva, Lifar, might lead in one ballet and be in the ensemble of the next, but now, of course, under the new dispensation they would not be recognised as stars. A star is an impresario's investment and must be continually in the limelight.

It is important to realise the true nature of ballet, for a volume of photographs is essentially a collection of stars, and the text alone can draw attention to the danger of an audience of " fans " watching stars with the mistaken idea that it is ballet that they are seeing.

It is interesting to see how the various nations reacted to the end of the Diaghileff regime, for the Diaghileff ballet was extra-territorial, composed of Russians in exile, Anglo-Russians and the artists and composers of Paris. I will deal with each phase in the appropriate place, but here are a few generalisations.

The new Russian Ballet, starting in 1932 from the old home at Monte Carlo, were the direct heirs. They started with the Diaghileff capital and goodwill which they succeeded in dissipating within five years. They quarrelled among themselves, enriched the legal profession, gave a bumper advertisement to the great little Principality, and then split into fragments, each one but a faint echo of the original. In vain one searches for new ideas. And yet there had never been more undeveloped dancing talent awaiting inspired leadership.

In England our ballet was started by Marie Rambert and by Ninette de Valois, also Diaghileff heirs, but poor relations in the sense that none of his repertoire was theirs and that they had to convince the public that " Russian Ballet " without Diaghileff was not the only safe brand. De Valois built the hard way round a small school and an unfashionable theatre, ignoring and at times rebuking her " fans." Her aim was to create the machinery of permanency and not to advertise premature results or to exploit stars. She gave Britain a national ballet; *a tremendous achievement.*

France had its Ballet at the Opéra, the oldest institution of all. For several generations it had stood still, attracting the country cousin to the front of the house and the elderly man about town to the *Foyer de la Danse*. If it justified itself at all, it was in having provided models for Degas—but then so did the washerwomen. The most genuine manifestation of the dance was the Carpeaux group that graced the façade. Lifar, a Diaghileff heir, came like Prince Charming and with a kiss awoke the dance to a vigorous life, introducing the Diaghileff artists, the Diaghileff public, and the Russian studio. Indirectly he had been responsible for the growth of other French companies, unofficial offshoots of the Opéra. Lifar re-created a national ballet for France; *a tremendous achievement.*

In America, in spite of the presence of Fokine and other Russian masters, ballet was completely despised—and rightly so since it had been relegated to picture houses and music halls—until the advent of de Basil in 1933-4. Gradually it began to gain in popularity, but frankly as an exotic ; the Russian label was an essential even if the dancer was a native of St. Petersburg, Fla., and the choreographer had found his inspiration in the Russian Tea Room. It was Balanchine, a Diaghileff heir, brought over and assisted by that cantankerous creative-enthusiast Lincoln Kirstein who inspired all the American efforts, starting with the School of American Ballet. He produced dancers of merit and developed a school of choreography; *a tremendous achievement.*

But the position in America differs greatly from that in England or France. The English Ballet has its own theatres and is semi-nationalised, the French Opéra Ballet has always been entirely nationalised, while Balanchine and Kirstein must battle in competition with the large commercial undertakings and their loud-mouthed publicity machines that are continually corrupting public taste; as well as with the over powerful unions that have so shameful a stranglehold on art.

That, then, is what has happened to the Diaghileff heritage.

THE NEW DANCER

The de Basil Ballet consisted of a skilled and highly successful mixture of the old and the new, the experienced and the tyro. To Danilova and Massine were added Toumanova, Baronova, Riabouchinska, Lichine, and Eglevsky. These last were the first of the new type of dancer to make a name in ballet—they not only made names for themselves, but contributed to the popularity of ballet wherever they danced. They represent something entirely new in the dance. This is not the place to discuss the talent of individuals but to set down some generalisations about the dancer: " model 1933 and after."

The new dancer is less of a specialist than her elder sister, who could much more easily be classified as ballerina, demi-caractère, or caractère. She tends far more to be a demi-caractère dancer, both by her training and by the fact that no company can afford narrow specialisation. The grand ballerina manner requires both time and a constant example in order to be acquired. Few of the dancers to-day have such an example in front of them; few, for instance, have seen that great ballerina Spessivtseva. The Russian revolution left a hiatus in the ballerina tradition, harmful to the new dancer, the new spectators, and the new critic.

The new dancer is more or less an individual from the start. That is to say, she does not resign herself as did so many of the dancers of former generations to a position in the back row of the corps de ballet. She has always the hope that a choreographer may find her physically or technically suited to some particular role in his next ballet. The result is that the corps de ballet is no longer so perfectly regimented as before. The modern girl finds corps de ballet work in *Swan Lake*, for instance, an intolerable bore. Modern choreography has taught her that there are other things to do besides being a piece of animated scenery. *Les filles de Mme. Cardinal* had in our grandfather's time the compensation of wealthy admirers.

The new dancer has an extensive if a by no means perfect technical equipment. She can do those pyrotechnics that once caused a sensation when performed by Legnani and which were regarded by the Diaghileff group as circus tricks. To-day they are a commonplace and—let us admit it—usually an insufferable bore though they always excite considerable applause. We seem at times to have returned to the pre-Diaghileff days of Minkus and Pugni with the *Don Quixote* pas de deux as a pièce de resistance. But if the pyrotechnics appear to succeed, very few dancers can walk across the stage in the grand manner, if the fouettés are multiplied indefinitely, they are by no means always correct. The dancer has not yet had the time fully to digest this classicism, to realize that virtuosity is a means and not an end.

Among these new generation dancers I have seen, three seem to me to have fulfilled themselves completely by harnessing technique to artistry and therefore to be undisputed ballerinas, Margot Fonteyn, Yvette Chauviré and Nina Vyroubova. Dancers, critics and public should study them; they set to-day's standards.

Yet in spite of the shortcomings there are undoubtedly to-day more dancers of undisputed talent and potentially great achievement than at any other period. Ballet has become a popular profession and the net has been cast wide to include girls of every class and race.

Let us be very careful, however, just because of the popularity of the profession, not to glamourize the dancer as the films would have us do. For every one artist there are dozens dancing to-day, competently enough, who are earning their living through practising a craft. They might have been typists, but they happened to have the physique of dancers. Glamour clouds all critical judgment. *Red Shoes* may be good cinema, it is certainly not a picture of dancing or dancers.

The above remarks apply also to the male dancer, though the Poles and Russians still retain an overwhelming supremacy. They have none of the tendency to the lack of virility that disfigures so much of contemporary ballet. They are still the Polovtsian warriors that aroused the Paris of 1910, driving away those amazons *en travesti* who made the art as ridiculous as a Christmas pantomime.

Even the romantic ballet, the rose or the poet in the churchyard, requires masculinity. The man is always the lover whether he wears long hair and a velvet jacket or Russian boots. We are too apt to confuse romanticism and effeminacy, to imagine that the real man is essentially a rather clumsy creature. Yet who more graceful than the hurdler, the sprinter, the diver or the cricketer ?

It is interesting to note the effect of nationality and environment on the new dancer and in consequence to modify some of these generalisations.

The new Russian dancer (*emigré*) has by now been largely absorbed into the French atmosphere and is culturally as well as in passport a French subject (e.g. Tcherina, Skorik, Vyroubova, Pagava), yet retains that fine carriage of head and shoulders and the wonderful extension of line so characteristic of the Russian school. She is not always accurate, often uneven in performance, but invariably she dances instead of performing a sequence of steps, also she possesses showmanship, and that does not mean the cheap trickery of an exaggerated preparation that takes the place of the drumbeats of the circus before the *salto mortale*. The English dancer is firmly based on the classics, has style, breeding, lyricism and a restraint that when it does not come from a lack of temperament is a positive quality. Because of this classical background she can still form part of a corps de ballet. She often fails through an over-conscientious approach in showmanship, presentation, attack and stagecraft. She is musical and not merely rhythmic. In roles that require definite acting she is second to none, since there she can hide her natural reserve behind a positive character.

The French dancer runs to extremes. She is either Lifar-inspired and a product of the studios of Preobrajenska, Kniaseff, Volinine, Egorova or Kchesinska, and therefore strongly Russian in influence; or belongs to an outmoded pre-Diaghileff academic tradition that is utterly ridiculous. One can almost feel the tightly-laced corset under the costume and the vapid grin is the same as the one Doré fixed for ever with his etching tool. The Lifar-inspired French dancer has been the revelation of the post-war years. She has the great strength that Lifar's choreography demands, and true finish. She brings to all her work a mature intelligence, realising the theatre aspect that lies behind classroom technique. She is essentially an individual and for that reason a French corps de ballet leaves much to be desired in its discipline and alignment. She is less musical than the English dancer, but makes her authority felt immediately. She wears and dances in the costume of any period superbly, but tends to be herself rather than any character she may be enacting.

The American dancer starts with a magnificent physical equipment and with an aptitude for technical difficulties that is astonishing. She can be absolutely anything required of her in a mechanical sense; indeed she can reduce the mechanics of dancing to so exact a science that they become boring and ridiculous. She has not, however, through lack of opportunity, understood the true classical style or the detail of the grand manner. A comparison between the dazzling Hightower and a Russian-schooled dancer of flawless classical style such as Nina Vyroubova, will make my point clear. Again, take the case of Nora Kaye, a really considerable artist, a subtle interpreter of character as we saw in the Tudor ballets that she created. She has a formidable technical equipment, but her classical roles reveal a lack of true classical feeling. The movements are hard, the line is clipped. The parody of the Russian School in *Gala Performance*—amusing as it undoubtedly is—shows a lack of comprehension of classicism. And yet, I repeat once again, Nora Kaye, interpreter of *Pillar of Fire, Jardin aux Lilas* or Juliet, is a very great artist.

The American dancer has a strong sense of rhythm, rather than an idea of musical phrasing. She dances with rare vitality. Though, inspired by Markova, she is in love with classicism, she interprets roles outside her immediate experience with a monotonous prettiness that makes the Polovtsian girl, the Russian nursemaid, or the houri, one with the bathing beauty. Even in ballet Hollywood rears its pretty-pretty permed head. The youthful New York City ballet will, I believe, lead in a new direction.

I am aware that there are endless exceptions to what I have written above, but taken *en masse* it stands as a true picture of the dancer of to-day.

CHOREOGRAPHY SINCE DIAGHILEFF

It is impossible to write clearly under this heading at the present time. Diaghileff had one choreographer at a time—in all his quarter-century but half a dozen— while to-day there are many and consequently there is no main discernible tendency. Even England's National Ballet enjoys the totally different approach of Ashton, de Valois and Helpmann. Only in France has Lifar reigned supreme for over fifteen years, though to-day his young disciples, Roland Petit and Janine Charrat, have gained their artistic majority. They are still somewhat over-dominated by the literary idea, but the impact of their work on a sophisticated audience is undoubted. Petit in particular, guided by Boris Kochno, has created a whole series of ballets not unworthy of the Diaghileff regime. The *ballet-russe* has largely been dominated by Leonide Massine, who launched the symphonic ballet—a choreographic bomb. The only new choreographer it has developed has been David Lichine, fertile in idea but ill provided for by his managements. In America Balanchine has been the main creative force, but the English Anthony Tudor, with his extremely personal and somewhat tortured approach, and the Americans, Agnes de Mille, Jerome Robbins and William Dollar, have had a decided influence. The last three have been inspired by the American scene and in *Fancy Free* Robbins has used the rather limited idiom with marked skill. It is rather outside ballet proper that America has truly expressed herself in the dance, through Martha Graham and that remarkable anthropologist-choreographer, Katherine Dunham.

There would appear to be two main and conflicting trends: the abstract "musical" ballet of Ashton and Balanchine and their disciples, and the dramatic *ballet d'action*, which is either neo-romantic, or expresses some contemporary concept in a modernist style.

The number of choreographers with their differing outlooks is, or should be, a healthy sign. Unfortunately, however, the budding choreographer has not the *ambiance* necessary for successful creation. There is no Diaghileff to guide and supervise; outside Paris no group of artists that has adopted ballet as a second art, and worse still, no time for the young dancer to educate himself.

From the choreographic point of view England is in a fortunate state. Ashton with such works as *Symphonic Variations* stands supreme in his conception of " danced music," inventive and original and yet avoiding both the extremes that degenerate into acrobacy and the over-subtleties of Balanchine, while the other tendency is brilliantly represented by de Valois who, with *Job, The Rake's Progress* and *Don Quixote*, has created undoubted masterpieces. Helpmann, still closer to the theatre, has in *Hamlet* and *The Miracle in the Gorbals*, solved the problem that the modern dance-theatre has so far only dabbled at in the form of danced propaganda leaflets.

This English success is, I am certain, largely due to the important position occupied in the repertoire by the classics. They supply the basic dance language, and whether they serve as an example or a standard from which to revolt, they inspire the choreographer.

MUSIC, DECOR AND LIBRETTO SINCE DIAGHILEFF

It is as difficult to write under this heading as it was under that of choreography and for the same reason. Not only can we no longer follow the evolution of an individual, but we are not dealing any more with deliberate policies, but with the workings of chance. What composer is available ? What painter can do something quickly ?

The ideal is an atmosphere in which artists can meet under the ægis of a gracious host, creative where people are concerned, and possessing a knowledge of all the arts, that inspires respect and confidence. Such was the atmosphere of Monte Carlo during Diaghileff's reign. When Fokine, Stravinsky, Cocteau, Bakst, Picasso, Benois and others are continually together, the result cannot fail to be a ballet that is perfectly balanced, a ballet conceived in such a way that it is impossible to say who hit upon the original idea. What could be more perfect than the union of de Falla and Picasso in *Le Tricorne*; Poulenc and Laurencin in *Les Biches* or Stravinsky and Goncharova in *Les Noces* ? The telephone or the week-end visit by plane after a frantic search for currency can never take the place of a leisurely discussion over a wine-laden supper table during a Mediterranean holiday.

To-day it is usually the choreographer himself who decides who shall be his next musical collaborator and who should then decorate the result. It is clearly not his function; he is one of a team, the specialist in movement. He cannot be *audessus de la melée*. While the post-Diaghilfor period has given us some good décors suitably wedded to music and choreography; with certain notable exceptions these have happened by good fortune rather than by design.

English ballet under the expert guidance of Constant Lambert has had a good musical record in commissioned works and an outstanding one in such brilliant arrangements as *Les Patineurs* from Meyerbeer, *Les Rendezvous* from Auber and

Apparitions from Liszt. In décor, however, it has fallen far below this level. Most of the ballets presented could have been given equally well in other settings; a mediocre good taste prevails; the great Russian insisted that there was nothing more sterile than " good taste." That in a non-classical ballet is, after all, the supreme test; could the ballet survive as the same work if given a different setting ? Think of *La Boutique Fantasque* or *Le Tricorne* and the answer is obvious. One new figure has emerged in Leslie Hurry and *Hamlet* would not be *Hamlet* without Hurry. His *Swan Lake* was not so successful; it never could have been, but it showed a deliberate design and was not the usual haphazard collection of amusingly pretty dresses against a sketchy background. He clearly needs guidance. Sophie Fedorovitch has always been perfectly suited to collaborate with Ashton and has given us a series of really distinguished sets. Burra and Bliss combine perfectly in *Miracle in the Gorbals* and Kauffer and Bliss in *Checkmate*, though here second thoughts were by no means the best. For the rest there is little that is positive. Derain's masterly colour orchestration for *Mam'zelle Angot* reveals the general poverty. He almost alone has made real use of the Opera House stage, a space that crushes the mediocre but enhances the true master of his art. What an opportunity was lost with the fairy world of *The Sleeping Beauty*, where Tchaikovsky's music itself paints the vast panorama!

The *ballet-russe* groups have followed the Diaghileff formula, have gone to his artists or their successors, but save under the guidance of Kochno it has been very much of a formula. The most distinguished de Basil sets have been Derain's *Concurrence*, Miro's *Jeux d'Enfants*, and Bérard's *Cotillon* and *Symphonie Fantastique* and Goncharova's *Coq d'Or*—a Diaghileff set this last. René Blum, a man of great taste, gave us a Derain masterpiece in *L'Epreuve d'Amour*. In America *ballet-russe* has used the immense talent of Tchelitcheff, the popular brilliance of Chagall who fills the stage so that the dancers become a luxury, the uninteresting romanticism of Berman and the expensive jocularities of the commercial Dali. For the rest we have mainly seen Diaghileff décors in utility versions. Musically *ballet-russe* has not commissioned one score of distinction.

It is to French ballet in general that we must look for outstanding decorative work and for ideas. True it is in the late Diaghileff manner, but then the late Diaghileff manner was entirely French. Bérard and Sauguet form an ideal alliance in *Les Forains*, Hugo and Ibert in *Les Amours de Jupiter*, Kosma and Brassai in *Le Rendezvous*, Pini and Françaix in *Les Demoiselles de la Nuit*. Wakhevitch has designed the only possible set for Cocteau's *Le Jeune Homme et la Mort*, Pierre Roy has dressed *Jeux de Cartes* with brilliance. And in the enormous frame of the Opéra, Cassandre, Bouchenne and others have designed in the grand and opulent Opera House manner. Moreover, in France the country of Gautier, the poet still plays a role in ballet. During one season alone, Claudel, Cocteau, Annouilh, have conceived subjects around which the artists could in harmony devise a ballet.

BALANCE-SHEET

It is largely a question of age, taste, and temperament, whether the conclusions to be drawn from this survey are optimistic or not, whether our balance-sheet shows a profit or a loss.

Gone is the perfection of detail in creation and execution that was the rule in the finest period of Serge Diaghileff, largely gone also is the desire to discover and to shock the public into a new understanding. The porcelain of *Carnaval* is sadly chipped, the sylphs are no longer as light as the brush strokes of a Corot, the Rose finds his way out of the window with more energy than grace, Bakst's bright butterfly wings are sadly tattered, the wit of *Les Biches* is no longer as astringent, and *Appolon Musagètes* has become a dancing exercise. On the other hand, ballet itself survives magnificently. We have Fonteyn, Chauviré and Vyroubova to make the gentle Giselle dance, suffer and die again; we have dancers of technique, artistry and personality in May, Grey, Jeanmaire, Marchand, Kriza, Shearer, Skorik; we have Babilée, Elvin, Skibine and our own protean Helpmann. I select at random; each person will make his own list according to his taste and experience. We can see such a variety of ballets as *Symphonic Variations, Job, Hamlet, Les Forains, Les Amours de Jupiter* and *Suite en Blanc* with *Le Jeune Homme et la Mort* to shock us as did once *l'Après Midi d'un Faune. Le Tricorne* and *La Boutique Fantasque* still have a vigorous life, and at Covent Garden also the classics live and are an inspiration. This whole period is commemorated in Baron's unique collection, the record of fifteen years, the most critical years in the history of a fragile and yet enduring art.

★   ★   ★   ★

This book is called *Baron at the Ballet,* an excellent descriptive title, since it presents the photographer's very personal experience as a ballet goer. The photographs selected are from a very large collection, but they do not pretend in any way to be a pictorial history. My role has in a sense been to " illustrate " Baron's pictures. This has not always been an easy task in spite of the wide range covered. I have tried to avoid writing notes and captions merely for the sake of filling so much space with black marks in order to make the book look pleasing. On some occasions I would have liked to have dealt with certain topics at greater length, on others I have found but little to say. It seems to me that when dealing with studies of some individual dancer, Baron himself can be far more revealing. So many collections of photographs have merely a few factual notes and some pleasant words about all concerned. Baron did not wish his book to follow this fashion. I have tried, therefore, to be as critical as the space and the occasion demanded, and, far more difficult, to be connected in thought about the very fertile period depicted. At times Baron may have held different opinions, as I might have chosen different subjects to record. We have, however, worked together in high good humour and have found more common ground than usual among ballet-goers. The gentlest of arts seems somehow to have raised the passions at every period in its history, and I have no doubt that this book will provide much fuel for discussion long after its subjects have laid aside their ballet shoes.

This introductory essay is dedicated to my friend and colleague Ursula Moreton, of Sadler's Wells, as a souvenir of our long friendship.

GISELLE

Giselle, which celebrated its centenary in 1941, is an admirable introduction to a nostalgic volume of ballet memories. It brings into first place the figure of Théophile Gautier, the Father of romantic ballet and with Diaghileff, the man who still dominates it from the tomb.

La Sylphide (p. 158) brought the great romantic movement into ballet, it " opened up for choreography," wrote Gautier, " a new era . . . the Opéra was surrendered to gnomes, undines, salamanders, wilis, pixies, péris and all those beings, strange and mysterious, who lend themselves so well to the fantasies of the maitre de ballet. The twelve marble and gold houses of the Olympians were relegated to the dust of the storehouses and only the romantic forests and valleys lit by the charming German moonlight of the ballads of Heinrich Heine exist."

La Sylphide was but the prelude to a greater and more enduring work.

Giselle, a ballet in two acts, was based by Gautier, St. George and Coralli, its choreographer on a theme suggested by Heinrich Heine. It's creator was Carlotta Grisi of whom Gautier wrote,

> " Carlotta Grisi most ably seconded by Petipa, has made the second act of the ballet a species of acting poem—a sort of choreographic elegy of the deepest pathos as well as elegant sentiment and more than one eye among the audience was dimmed with a tear, when expectation had only looked for admirable dancing."

He could never look upon another Giselle with complete approval. It is fascinating to speculate what touches of Grisi remain with Giselle today.

Giselle presents an exception to the rule that the life of a ballet is dictated by the quality of its music. *Giselle* was created in 1841 and is included in every company's repertoire, although Adam's music, an advance in its day, is of no interest on its own. The reason for its long life is Théophile Gautier's inspired choice of a theme. *Giselle* is a dramatically compact example of all that is finest in romantic ballet. Each of its two acts has a theme, the first the body, the second the spirit. Moreover the first scene has sharp contrasts of mood between carefree innocent gaiety and a deep sorrow that finishes in madness and suicide. There is everything there for the dramatic ballerina to express with the added difficulty for the contemporary dancer that it must all be kept within the framework of a definite period, one so very different from our own.

In discussing *Giselle* we must be very careful in our use of terms. *Giselle* which is the very essence of romanticism, is often called a classical ballet. Dramatically, musically and scenically it is romantic—especially when the wilis are made fly— but the dance technique is classical. Its interpreter, therefore, among other essentials requires the impeccable technique of the *ballerina assoluta*.   Is it to be wondered at that no two critics can agree on the perfect Giselle; perhaps no perfect Giselle exists !   The perfect Giselle might be a composite figure made up of three dancers, the gay, the tragic and the aetherial.   For that reason alone this centenarian is still the most discussed of works and indispensable in the repertoire of the ballerina.   It might almost be said to give her letters patent to the title.   The male role of Albrecht is also of interest in spite of the period of the work, and Gautier's known dislike of the male dancer.   Nijinsky showed the full possibilities of the part and in our time Lifar has been a magnificent Albrecht.   The short scene where he finds his way into the wood to lay the lilacs on Giselle's grave, a walk across the stage, wrapped in a trailing purple cloak will never be forgotten by those who saw the remarkable series of performances with Spessivtseva at the Paris Opéra.

Within present balletic memories Pavlova, Karsavina, Spessivtseva, Markova, Fonteyn, Chauviré, Toumanova, Darsonval and Vyroubova have each contributed something that brought life to Gautier's conception.

The second dancing role, the Queen of the Wilis, is in many ways a thankless one. It calls for a technique of strength, brilliance and endurance, and for a strong personality yet one that must be completely overshadowed the moment that Giselle rises from the tomb.   Ruth French, Danilova, Beryl Grey and Marjorie Tallchief are dancers one remembers here.

Gautier saw the role of Princess Bathilde as an important one, an essential dramatic contrast to the unsophisticated girl.   He even wrote a poem " à la Princesse Bathilde " :

> " *Alors vous paraissez, chasseresse superbe*
> *Trainant votre velours sur le velours de l'herbe* ".

Alas, today the role usually passes for nothing and the contrast is lost.   Ursula Moreton is the one Bathilde I can remember to whom Gautier's poem might apply.

There remain the villain, a conventional role of melodrama, *ham* in the grand manner, that must be played full out and with conviction and Giselle's mother, who is too often for no known reason presented as senile and doddering.   At most she cannot have been much older than thirty-six, an energetic peasant woman.

Baron has left us a record of a number of Giselles, doing for our generation what the lithographers Brandard and others did for Giselle's own.   The record may be more exact but to me something is missing, the awe with which an audience once looked at a Grisi, something that emerges so clearly from the naive and in no sense realistic lithographs of these very minor artists.   Since there can clearly be no self-conscious return to such modes of expression I welcome the camera's record.

Two notable productions shown in some detail are those of the René Blum Ballet de Monte Carlo, Drury Lane, 1939 with Markova, Lifar and Danilova as Queen of the Wilis, pages 28 and 29, and of Sadler's Wells at Covent Garden in 1947 with Fonteyn, Rassine and Grey, pages 30 and 31.   It will be seen from this last production how the old device of the flying wilis adds to the illusion.

MARGOT FONTEYN as *Giselle*

p. 28 and 29.   *Giselle* Act II.   p. 28 MARKOVA and LIFAR.   p. 29 MARKOVA with
DANILOVA as Queen of the Wilis and the Ensemble.   (*Monte Carlo Ballet ; Drury*
Lane 1939).
p. 30 and 31.   *Giselle* Act II.   The flying Wilis, FONTEYN and RASSINE.   GREY as
Queen of the Wilis.   p. 31 GREY as Queen of the Wilis and the Ensemble.   (*Sadler's Wells*
revival, Covent Garden 1946.   Costumes and décors by James Bailey).

31

MARGOT FONTEYN
Baron reveals a magnificent moment of Fonteyn's artistry in what is a
fine example of a posed action study referred to in his introduction.

(*Opposite*) ALICIA MARKOVA in *Giselle* Act II

ALICIA MARKOVA as Giselle in a study that recalls the romantic lithographs.   The lightness of Markova's second act is unique.   *Taken* 1948.

*Giselle and Albrecht who woos
her incognito*

TAMARA TOUMANOVA made her début as
Giselle at Drury Lane in 1939. She was then too
immature to see beyond the technical possibilities
of the role. Today she gives a magnificently
reasoned performance in which only the simplicity
of Giselle's entrance and early happiness escape
her. In the scene of 'douce folie' and in the second
act she can, when fully controlled, give a truly
magnificent interpretation in which the virtuoso is
the servant of the actress.

She is here seen with IGOR YOUSKEVITCH,
an outstanding Russian dancer who began to make
a name before the war but whose main career has
been in the U.S.A.

Giselle takes pity on Albrecht, exhausted in his 'dance of death'

TAMARA TOUMANOVA AND IGOR YOUSKEVITCH

Toumanova was then $16\frac{1}{2}$ years old. This company, under the direction of René Blum had two great Giselles in Toumanova and Markova, and two outstanding Albrechts in Lifar and Youskevitch. *Taken on the stage of Drury Lane Theatre in 1939.*

YVETTE CHAUVIRE AND SERGE LIFAR
The great French ballerina's interpretation is closer to the spirit of the old prints than any other and consequently closer to the period as revealed in the music. This is a French ballet, a part of the Opéra tradition, as Chauviré, most outstanding French ballerina since the romantic period, so clearly shows.

(*Above*) MARINA FRANKA as one of the leading Wilis.   *Taken on the stage at Drury Lane in 1939, Ballet Russe de Monte Carlo.*

MARKOVA AND YOUSKEVITCH

SALLY GILMOUR as the Giselle of Act I

Marie Rambert's version of *Giselle* has been highly acclaimed for its dramatic verity. Sally Gilmour gains our sympathy from the curtain rise and establishes the character of Giselle. The lack of a ballerina's classical attack, however, interferes with the complete presentation of the role.

MARGOT FONTEYN

" Among women," says Gautier, " reason is in the heart; wounded heart, damaged brain. Giselle loses her reason; not that she lets her hair fall in disorder and strikes her forehead in the manner of the heroine of a melodrama; hers is a gentle madness, as tender and charming as she herself."

Margot Fonteyn brings extraordinary warmth and humanity to the role, stressing the tenderness upon which Gautier insists.

Taken on the stage at Covent Garden Opera House in 1946.

FROM GAUTIER TO COCTEAU

Romanticism to Decadence

In France the poet has always played a major role in ballet production. *Giselle* and its whole period are far more closely associated with Théophile Gautier than with any single choreographer. That tradition has persisted in France. The Diaghileff Ballet with its spiritual headquarters in Paris owed much to the poets Vaudoyer, Cocteau and Kochno. There is in France no great barrier between the arts. Practically every writer of note has published a volume of art or musical criticism. French thought, always logical, tends to run in schools that comprise all the arts; impressionism, surrealism, apply equally to painting, music and verse.

This means that at the same time ballet is taken both more and less seriously than over here. More seriously since it interests poets, dramatists, painters and composers as much as choreographers who use it to express the idea of the moment. Less seriously at times just because it is the idea of the moment that they seek to express, and the idea of the moment does not often hold the stage for more than a season or two.

In theory, theme, music, choreography and décor are equal partners. Fokine laid that down and it is the basis of modern ballet. In practice, however, we in England tend to stress the choreography and dancing, while France underlines the theme.

French balletic ideas have never failed to enrich the art. But although the Diaghileff Ballet was Franco-Russian, French dancing and choreography were almost non-existent. The Opéra for many years justified its existence through providing ' rats ' for the brush of Dégas or a Mademoiselle Cardinal for a wealthy protector. It was the advent of Serge Lifar in 1931 as premier danseur, maître de ballet and choreographer that brought an example and a serious purpose to French ballet. His work lay hidden to the world outside Paris for over a decade, but then to the Frenchman there is no world outside Paris. In Britain and America Lifar's work is still insufficiently known either in quality, direction or extent. Were it known it might not find favour, but that is another matter. What we do know however is the work of his young disciples, those who found a vocation through his teaching and example. Among them Roland Petit ranks very high. He first showed us his work, at the Adelphi Theatre with Les Ballets des Champs Elysées in 1946, the first post-war visit of a foreign company to Britain. Since then we have had a yearly visit from this company and from Roland Petit's new venture, Les Ballets de Paris.

Les Ballets des Champs Elysées owes its artistic policy to Diaghileff's lieutenant Boris Kochno, the most Parisian of Russians and most Russian of Parisians.

Kochno's outlook has not changed since the 1920's. He has a profound admiration for classicism but he says " it is not for a travelling company such as ours. I do not want to repeat *Les Sylphides* indifferently year after year. I want to express something new and as soon as it ceases to be new I want to forget it."

That point of view, which we must always bear in mind so that we do not commit the critical sin of comparing dissimilar organisations, results in shock tactics designed to make an immediate impact. It means the sacrifice of corps de ballet discipline and of company homogeneity. The accent is on the individual who can be used to create a particular effect, such as the inspired acrobatics of a Darmance or the physique of a Caron, so closely identified with the Bérard Sphinx.

Most outstanding and typical of these shock tactics works is *Le Jeune Homme et la Mort*. It is very definitely a shocker. Its theme by Jean Cocteau is very much the French theme of the moment, the preoccupation with death that the poet has shown in his *L'Aigle à Deux Têtes* and other works. Death woos the disillusioned young artist with brutality. Finally he gives in to her and hangs himself. Then in an apotheosis she takes him out of the dirty garret and into the clear night above *la ville lumière*.

Stated bluntly this is a rather sordid *fait divers* from the columns of *Samedi Soir*. Cocteau has however wedded it to Bach's *passacaglia in C*. It would at first seem impossible to have chosen more unsuitable music and if the music critic rejects it with indignation, he is perfectly within his rights. But dramatically this very contrast is magnificently effective. The passionate logic of the music underlines the passionate dementia of the young man, showing us the depth of his despair. Music and action only meet in the apotheosis.

As always in French productions the scenic artist, Wakhevitch, contributes to the drama so completely that one cannot separate his work from Petit's choreography.

The dancing of Nathalie Phillipart and Jean Babilée will be remembered as long as that of Karsavina and Nijinsky in the tender *Le Spectre de la Rose*. This belongs to our times, as *Le Spectre de la Rose* to the pre-1914 era, says Kochno.

If I have headed this section " from Romanticism to Decadence," it is not to attack this particular work but to situate it as belonging to the tail end of romanticism. *Giselle* also tells of betrayal and suicide but its setting is remote from our everyday experience, its hero is a Prince while Le Jeune Homme is a disillusioned artist we might meet in any Montparnasse café. He lives in a garret that we have all seen, and even in the final apotheosis in his progress to the other world we meet with the familiar word CITROEN flashed from a sign on the Eiffel Tower.

Is it a ballet at all? I cannot say and I do not care. It is today tremendously effective theatre, tomorrow it may seem as dead as Aunt Fanny's feather boa. Baron has fixed its essentials in a magnificent series of photographs.

Le Jeune Homme et la Mort

JEAN BABILEE as le jeune homme bored and disillusioned in his garret
as the curtain rises. *Taken on the stage at the Winter Garden Theatre in 1947*

43

Death (NATHALIE PHILLIPART) woos the young man (JEAN BABILEE)

The struggle between Death and the young man, expressed in a violent acrobatic idiom in which the crash of the furniture hurled across the studio contrasts with the logical development of Bach's music until the nervous tension grows almost unbearable. Throughout this brutal courtship Death is in complete control, first cajoling then spurning. One can feel that the young man's very violence in his efforts to escape is a sign of weakness and that the end is inevitable.

Jean Cocteau, artist, poet and dramatist, has made greater use of the ballet medium than any other writer since Gautier. He began his association with Diaghileff as a very young man in 1912, three years after the Russian invasion, with a poster and a brochure, and remained a collaborator till the end. He contributed the theme for *Le Dieu Bleu* (1913), *Parade* (1917), *Le Train Bleu* (1924). He also wrote notable works for Les Ballets Suèdois and for the Opéra, notably *Phèdre* for Lifar in 1950.

Characteristically his choice of music for *Le Jeune Homme et la Mort* was kept a secret from all save the conductor until the première, the ballet being rehearsed to swing rhythms.

Death knots the noose on the cross beam (*left*) and hurries out of the room (*right*) knowing that she has gained a victory.

Jean Babilée's *Jeune Homme* attracts the lion's share of the attention just as did Nijinsky's spectre in *Le Spectre de la Rose*. It would however be impossible to imagine a finer or more subtle performance than Phillipart's brutally tender death. This dancer has not a strong classical technique; it is as an actress that she excels, an actress in every muscle of her body. Her entrance into the studio as she stands in the doorway quivering with passion, is one of the strongest moments in modern French ballet with its decadence that excels in such purple passages. Only Phillipart and Babilée have danced this work; it is inconceivable without them.

A final flicker of life, the spasmodic movement of a dying animal and the youth, so violent and full of life, finds peace.

THE RUSSIAN RENAISSANCE
1933-1939

The Russians themselves have never seen what we in Western Europe call Russian Ballet. It was the work of expatriates who conquered the whole world but who could not prevail against the diehard attitude of their own balletomanes. At the height of the Russian Revolution, Diaghileff shocked the Soviet poet Maya-kovksy with Massine's revolutionary *Le Pas d'Acier*. The Russian Ballet in Russia was an institution, in the rest of the world it was a man, Serge Diaghileff. When he died it seemed unlikely that it would survive. "The puppet master is dead. Put the toys away," wrote a French critic. Russian Ballet, however, had a greater vitality than this critic allowed. It was born again at Monte Carlo in 1932 under the direction of René Blum and Colonel W. de Basil.

On July 4th, 1933, it came to London for the first of six visits. With it began the era of balletomania and the complete democratisation of the art in its long journey from Versailles. The company was admirably composed of experienced and new elements. Balanchine, Massine, Tchernicheva, Danilova Woizikovski and Grigorieff's phenomenal memory backed up the instinctive artistry of the ' babies,' Baronova, Toumanova and Riabouchinska, Verchinina, Lichine and Eglevsky. Public relations departments for the first time added two or three years to the age of their stars. The Monte Carlo Ballet started with such magnificent creations as Balanchine's *Cotillon* and Massine's *Jeux d'Enfants*. They gave us with *Les Présages* and *Choreartium* the fierce controversy of the symphonic ballet, in which Ernest Newman lent the weight of his authority to the symphonists. Who will forget those warm summer evenings ending with the gaiety of *Le Beau Danube* or the excitement of Leon Woizikovski and his Polovtsian bowmen ?

It was a complete renaissance. We took its return for granted, feverishly applaud-ing each Aurora variation on its first night. Unfortunately it took its own existence for granted, drawing more and more heavily on the Diaghileff repertoire and giving its young dancers less and less time to assimilate its subtleties.

Let us be quite fair. Economics play their part. Diaghileff could find a backer when driven to the wall, de Basil must play all the year round to keep his large company alive. Months and months of one night stands in America. The stars grow to believe the ' puffs ' of their own publicity men and then ask themselves why they should travel so much when Broadway is so much more comfortable and lucrative. There is glory and money for dancers and personalities clash. Soon there are two, then three rival companies, but the talent is not doubled or trebled. Only the posters grow larger, the names appear in bigger print and the journeys are as long as ever. It is a marvel in this period if the painter, composer and choreographer can confer more than a month before the first night. Ballets are created by cable instead of round the table at the Savoy or Hotel de Paris.

The climax is reached in 1939, the de Basil Ballet appearing as usual at Covent Garden and a new Monte Carlo Ballet at Drury Lane. Some balletomanes made up their evening's programme from both houses. The essential difference between the original ballet russe of 1909 and this brief though brilliant renaissance does not however, lie merely in economics. Diaghileff used ballet to present ideas, his successor presented ballet. Diaghileff gave the public what he wanted, his successor what he thought the public wanted. Diaghileff made great use of publicity but in a far more subtle manner. Doubtless after the succés de scandale of *L'après midi d'un faune* (1912) and *Le Sacre du Printemps* (1913) he not only savoured such publicity but that he took a hand in provoked it. This publicity was not centred round legs but ideas. He could enlist the pen of a Rodin. His taste was what mattered and his dancers, however great, occupied a subordinate position. Much publicity was focussed on Nijinsky but, when Nijinsky finally left, the ballet went on to fresh ideas and fresh triumphs. It survived the loss of Fokine, Massine and Lopokova. No subsequent Russian company could afford such losses.

In the new Russian Ballet ideas no longer mattered, the limelight was centred on dancers alone and when, through the loss of dancers, the impresario received a large share of publicity, nobody cared because he was not associated with the artistic life of his times. Diaghileff took a moribund art and enlisted on its behalf the first artistic minds of his period, guiding and influencing them. He knew exactly when to change direction from Bakst and Benois via Larionov to Picasso and Derain. The new Ballet Russe stood still, brilliantly it is true, until those who had been unable to follow Diaghileff caught up with it, gathering to itself an enormous public. But it continued to stand still, no longer able to advance.

Yet Ballet owes much to Colonel de Basil. He extended its frontiers, he started both its popularity and its practice in the United States. Before his visit to the St. James's Theatre in 1933 ballet was associated with big picture palace presentations. I once saw a ballet called *Schéhérazade* in which an elephant appeared in a heavy character role. De Basil brought the unfamiliar Diaghileff repertoire to America, training future dancers, a vast public and a group of first class critics.

Alas, Western European Russian Ballet, or Ballet Russe, as one critic has aptly called it, is a thing of the past. The great teachers who formed it have grown old, the little emigrées are almost completely French or American in education and outlook. The future belongs to the national ballets or the smaller and more mobile groups. And more is the pity, for Monte Carlo with its leisured cosmopolitan atmosphere had something invaluable to contribute to the art. It was the logical rallying ground for the rebels from the more conservative opera house schools.

(*Opposite*) IRINA BARONOVA and ANTON DOLIN in David Lichine's *Le Fils Prodigue* to Prokofieff's score and Rouault's décor. *Taken on the stage at Drury Lane in* 1939

NINA VERCHININA, dancer of *Les Présages* and *Choreartium* in which Massine
combined ballet and modern dance techniques.

54

Le Coq D'Or

ALGERANOFF as The Magician

One of the most Russian and exotic of the de Basil creations was *Le Coq D'Or*, a danced version of Rimsky-Korsakoff's opera with striking settings by Nathalie Gontcharova (*Covent Garden* 1937).

This had first been produced by Diaghileff in 1914, the opera being sung by singers massed at the sides and danced by the company led by Karsavina as the Queen of the Shemakhan. Both versions were by Michael Fokine.

IRINA BARONOVA'S Queen of Shemakhan was one of her outstanding creations and the scene in which she mocked the amorous King Dodon had both wit and humour as well as warmth and sympathy.

Baronova had by now grown out of her 'baby star' phase and was a conscious artist with a wide range.

(*Left*) SONO OSATO in *Le Coq D'Or*. This dancer, half Irish-American, half Japanese, attracted considerable attention in such small roles as the Odalisque in *Schéhérazade* and in a similar role in the ballet shown here. It was inevitable with so striking a physique that she should be cast to type but in every role she danced with great intelligence.

(*Right*) MARK PLATOFF as Malatesta in David Lichine's *Francesca da Rimini*.

This young American dancer, who later found his way into films, was a fine interpreter of character roles. *Francesca da Rimini* was not an outstanding ballet but it had a melodramatic vitality that kept it in the repertoire. The music by Tchaikowsky, though made up from his symphonic poems was perfectly suited to such dramatic interpretation and at times carried it to a pitch of real excitement. Tchernicheva's Francesca and Platoff's Malatesta were roles that could easily have been ridiculous without the artistry that they were given.

This ballet marked the return to creation of Lubor Tchernicheva who, though no longer young, since she had danced with Diaghileff from his early years, interpreted the role of a girl of 16 in a manner that carried conviction.

Paganini

This was the last pre-war creation of the de Basil Ballet and the last Fokine première directed by the Master himself that London was to see. It was danced to the music of the Paganini-Rachmaninoff Variations and decorated by Soudeikine. It had a mixed reception. It was for the most part a thoroughly conventional work. Outstanding were a dance by Riabouchinska, her greatest creation without a doubt, Baronova's angel (pictured below) and Dimitri Rostoff's miming in the title role (shown opposite). These gave flashes of the real Fokine but in the rest he had gone back to the romantic paraphernalia that he had discarded in his own *Les Sylphides*.

There can be no doubt that, masterly choreographer though he was, the father of modern choreography, Fokine's greatest works, with the exception of the enchanting *L'épreuve d'amour*, were created under the guidance of Diaghileff whose critical judgment proved so important in the case of *Les Sylphides*.

59

In 1939 a new Monte Carlo company came to Covent Garden. These photographs show LEONIDE MASSINE in two contrasting roles, in rehearsal as St. Francis in Hindemith's *Nobilissima Visione*, a difficult work that repaid study and as the Peruvian with MIA SLAVENSKA in the gay but obvious *Gaieté Parisienne* to an Offenbach pot-pourri.

Petrouchka remains the greatest of all dramatic ballets, one that is so Russian in spirit that only a Russian company can interpret it.   Above, the Polish dancer, Yura Lazovsky, who began to attract critical attention shortly before the war is seen in the title role.
Taken in the studio in 1939

THE SADLER'S WELLS BALLET
Birth of an English Tradition

Sadler's Wells started courageously in the lull between the death of Diaghileff and the appearance of Colonel de Basil.   For sometime it seemed to the general public a background for the enchanting Markova.   Only when she left in 1935 to form her own company could Miss de Valois' work be assessed at its true value.   She had started an English school of ballet.   Today that may seem a simple and obvious statement, then it was far from simple.   Then the phrase 'going to the ballet' meant the Russian Ballet, today it means the Sadler's Wells Ballet.   That is the only way in which we can measure Miss de Valois' creation, the whole of which has been a triumph of long term planning in which immediate box office advantage has never been allowed to interfere with the integrity of the whole.

Today the Sadler's Wells Ballet under the direction of its founder has its first company at Covent Garden, its second at Sadler's Wells and its own school at Baron's Court.   Its dancers have a recognised style of their own and form a matchless ensemble.   From that " school " stars such as Fonteyn and Helpmann have emerged.   It has in its repertoire the classics in their entirety and creations of its own choreographers, Frederick Ashton, Ninette de Valois and Robert Helpmann.

FREDERICK ASHTON
Principal Choreographer

NINETTE DE VALOIS
Director

CONSTANT LAMBERT
Musical Director

The word 'school' is particularly important here in terms of the history of ballet.   We can clearly recognise the French school, though in its undiluted form it is almost obsolete, and the Italian school also is something definite, though the genius of Cecchetti has modified it considerably.   We are most familiar with the Russian school, product of France and Italy brought about through the work of Petipa, Johannsen and Cecchetti on the naturally gifted Russians.   The formation of these schools has taken several generations, the Russian school itself only coming to full perfection at the beginning of the century and reaching its fullest development with Olga Spessivtseva in the 1920's, that is as far as non-Russian spectators are concerned. Have we had time yet for an English school and what exactly is involved ?

The foundations of a school were laid by the Russians, by the example of Pavlova and the Diaghileff Ballet and by the direct teaching of Cecchetti, Astafieva and Legat. Ninette de Valois, the conscious founder of the English school, was a prominent soloiste of the Diaghileff Ballet and a pupil of Cecchetti. The first ballerina of Sadler's Wells, Alicia Markova, was trained by Astafieva and had her first experience with Diaghileff. The English school therefore is firmly Russian-based. Moreover a feature of its repertoire is the classical ballet of Petipa that first formed the Russian dancer. In that respect, and it is important, its roots go back further than from the first coming of the Russians to Western Europe. The modifications of the Russian school that will form an unmistakable English school will come about through the temperament and physique of some generations of English dancers. It has been said that the English dancer is over disciplined. This is not accurate. Self discipline is an English characteristic. Discourage it and you will get mannerism rather than true personality. Restraint and a fine ensemble are already, for better or for worse, characteristics of the new school.

The Sadler's Wells Ballet is sometimes called the National Ballet and with good reason. But in art an insistence on nationality can be dangerous. Serge Diaghileff was a Russian patriot. He collected the works of Russian authors, he assembled the painting of his country, he made a mission of showing Russian art to Western Europe. Yet the entirely Russian works of his Russian Ballet were few. *Prince Igor*, *Petrouchka*, *The Midnight Sun*, *Children's Tales* and *Les Noces* are those that come to mind out of a repertoire of over fifty works. The Sadler's Wells Ballet takes the same wide view of nationality. It is as British as Diaghileff was Russian yet its specifically native inspired works are not many and do not owe their place in the repertoire to deliberate policy. The company has called on a wider range of choreography than any other ; Massine, Balanchine, Petit have been invited to enrich it, as well as painters and composers from the continent.

The Three Cornered Hat

Perhaps the greatest monument to Diaghileff's international outlook was the Spanish ballet *The Three Cornered Hat*. It stands as a model of ballet creation in which all the arts are equal partners in the final result. Manuel de Falla has taken the folk music of Spain and translated it into terms of ballet music to be played by a symphony orchestra, Pablo Picasso has taken the traditional folk costume and translated it to the use of the ballet stage and Leonide Massine has done the same with the popular dances. Three creators but a perfectly unified result that is as fresh as the day it was created and that in the sense of its timelessness is a classic.

The Three Cornered Hat had its première at the Alhambra Theatre, London, in 1917. Its principal roles were created by Tamara Karsavina and Leonide Massine. These roles have since been danced by Lubov Tchernicheva, Lydia Sokolova and Tamara Toumanova and Leon Woizikovsky in the de Basil revival. At Sadler's Wells the revival was created by Margot Fonteyn and Leonide Massine and the roles have also been danced by Violetta Elvin, Harold Turner and Michael Somes.

LEONIDE MASSINE as The Miller in *The Three Cornered Hat* Created in 1917, revived in 1947. These dates are difficult to believe. Massine's vitality remains unimpaired, his artistry has grown.

LEONIDE MASSINE AND MARGOT FONTEYN

The first night of this ballet's revival by Sadler's Wells at Covent Garden on 6th Feb. 1947 was one of the most memorable occasions in the company's history. It revealed even to those who knew and admired the Wells a capacity that they had not believed possible in British dancers. This time they were challenging comparison with a great company of the past and memory always plays against the present. The impact of Massine on the company was tremendous and will never be forgotten by those who were present.

LEONIDE MASSINE in the Farucca

It was during the 1914 war, while with Diaghileff in Spain, that Massine learnt the Spanish and gypsy dancing that he was to interpret as choreographer and dancer with such success that his work gained acclaim in Spain, a country notoriously jealous of its native art. This photograph shows the quality of Massine's dancing, his ability to make a lack of motion into something positive and exciting, a vivid contrast to the dance that follows.

(*Opposite*) LEONIDE MASSINE; viewed from an electrician's perch rehearsing *The Three Cornered Hat*.

Symphonic Variations

Frederick Ashton's ballet to the music of César Franck, first produced for Sadler's Wells at Covent Garden in 1947, is a choreographic interpretation of the music. The aim is 'visual music' and the story element is omitted. In ballet of this type the décor and costumes are of great importance. They must not suggest character or period but they must be positive, they must parallel the mood of the music. The collaboration between Frederick Ashton, Choreographer, and Sophie Fedorovitch, Designer, has been complete.
The dancers here depicted are MOIRA SHEARER, MICHAEL SOMES, PAMELA MAY and MARGOT FONTEYN.

MOIRA SHEARER, MARGOT FONTEYN, MICHAEL SOMES and HENRY DANTON. *Taken on the stage at Covent Garden Opera House in* 1946

Such ballets of musical interpretation, the much used 'abstract' is a misleading term, call for dancers who are sensitive musicians and who can subordinate their personalities more completely than in any classical or character role.

Dante Sonata

Dante Sonata, a ballet with a theme of conflict and suffering set by
Frederick Ashton to the music of Liszt, was first produced at
Sadler's Wells in 1940. The costumes and setting, after Flaxman,
designed by Sophie Fedorovitch.
The dancers are (*left*) MARGOT FONTEYN and (*right*) PAMELA
MAY. (*Opposite*) JUNE BRAE and ROBERT HELPMANN.
*Picture on right was taken in 1939, on the stage at the Sadler's
Wells Theatre*

Les Sirènes

Les Sirènes, a light-hearted frolic by Frederick Ashton with settings by Cecil Beaton, and music by Lord Berners, was over-elaborate as a joke and completely out of place in the Opera House setting. Moreover, its Edwardian nostalgia had already been fully exploited in the more suitable medium of the revue.

FREDERICK ASHTON is here shown as an Eastern potentate in one of the wittiest scenes in the ballet.
Taken on the stage at Covent Garden in 1946

Adam Zero

ROBERT HELPMANN'S *Adam Zero*, music Arthur Bliss and décor by Roger Furse, uses the stage resources of Covent Garden to symbolise in Ballet form the destiny of man. In a ballet that varied from real strength to banality Robert Helpmann as the Man at all his ages and June Brae as the Mother, the Woman and Death were outstanding. They are shown on this page and the two that follow.

75

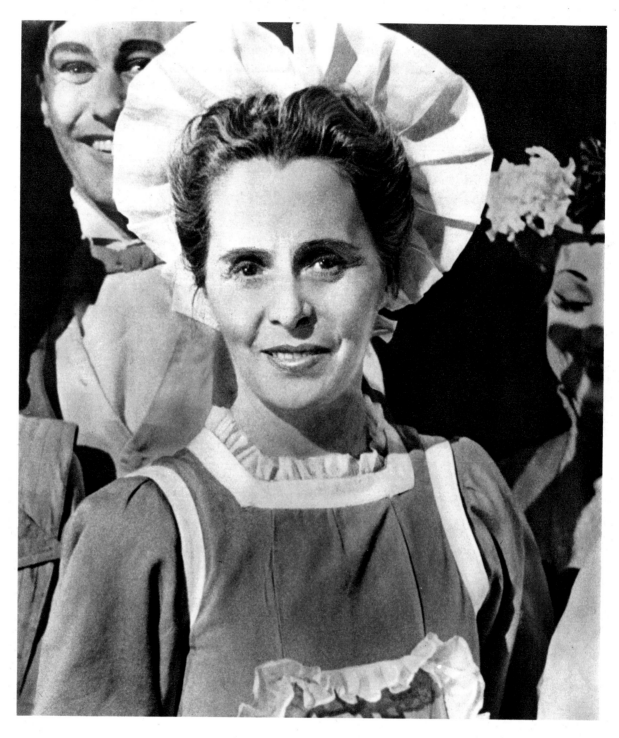

Ninette de Valois in A Wedding Bouquet

This photograph of Ninette de Valois was taken on the stage of the Sadler's Wells Theatre at the Gala Performance held to celebrate the twenty-first anniversary of the Sadler's Wells Ballet on May 15th, 1950.

A GALLERY OF BRITISH PORTRAITS

Commentary on these portraits is difficult. Only the ballerina is complete. The young dancer in particular varies so from season to season that a text would be unfair both to dancer and critic. These portraits must and do speak for themselves.

PEARL ARGYLE a pioneer of British Ballet and a première danseuse both with Marie Rambert and Sadler's Wells. Her beauty, serenity, poise and maturity at a time when our ballet was young and unacclaimed, ensure her an important place in its history and an unforgettable place in our memories.

MARKOVA

Alicia Markova is a dancer of four distinct careers; a child of promise with Diaghileff, a star and a pioneer with British ballet, both with Rambert, Sadler's Wells and her own company, ballerina of a Russian company in America and now with her brilliant partner Anton Dolin, the only 'concert ballerina' to draw a mass public.

Emotionally Markova has developed late. Her early reputation was built on ease and lightness. Today she is heir to Pavlova in *The Dying Swan* and her prelude in *Les Sylphides* is sensitively musical as it never was before. Her *Giselle*, depicted on these pages is unique in its second act.

FONTEYN

MARGOT FONTEYN in *Apparitions*

In countries where there is a state ballet the title *ballerina* is as official as that of general, the dancer is in fact a civil servant and a definite salary is attached to the function.   In England and America the title is a courtesy one and is greatly misused as a consequence.   To be a ballerina a dancer must not only dance the leading roles in the classical repertoire ; she must really interpret them in a personal way.   She must in fact enrich the tradition from which she has received so much.

(*Overleaf*) MARGOT FONTEYN as *Cinderella*

The photographs on this page show Fonteyn in a bare foot, plastically conceived role in ' Dante Sonata ' where the classical ballerina becomes part of a pattern.

A ballerina is born and not made, though a potential ballerina can be ruined by bad teaching. A ballerina is a rare being. In its greatest period the Maryinsky produced but few among its many great dancers; Kehessinska, Preobrajenska, Trefilova, Pavlova, Karsavina.

The travelling ballet company, however brilliant its repertoire, does not produce the ballerina. The Opera House is her cradle, the full length classic her great opportunity. Remove from the repertoire for only ten years *Swan Lake*, *The Sleeping Beauty* and *Giselle* and the Ballerina would be a thing of the past. A company can exist and can create without the ballerina, but the ballerina cannot exist outside the company.

MARGOT FONTEYN in *Giselle*

Margot Fonteyn is the first ballerina to be produced out of our own ballet tradition. She emerged in 1935 when Markova left Sadler's Wells to lead her own company.

As will be seen from the following pages she has extraordinary versatility; a versatility only matched by Tamara Karsavina. Fonteyn is today a classical ballerina of real authority and like the greatest her strong technique is subordinated to the needs of the music and the role. It is interesting to see how she develops a role from season to season, the detail that she brings to a familiar part is amazing, yet the detail does not intrude and it is the whole that one applauds.

There are certain episodes in Fonteyn's

MARGOT FONTEYN in Frederick Ashton's *Apparitions*. Dress designed by Cecil Beaton.

interpretation of the classics that lend a rich humanity to what is so often stereotyped. Watch the moment when Aurora pricks her finger. Here is a scene that often passes for nothing. Fonteyn gives us the hurt surprise of the sheltered only child and the desire to be comforted and then the moment of real fear before she swoons. When in that same ballet she makes her first entrance she immediately establishes the character which penetrates the presence of the great ballerina. Next when she dances the *Rose Adagio* instead of the rather tortured acrobatics of even some good dancers here is a girl meeting her suitors and by a glance including her parents in the scene. With Fonteyn the dance becomes a part of the drama.

To me one of her greatest triumphs is in Ashton's musical masterpiece *Symphonic Variations* where the ballerina must deliberately play down her personality to become one of a group. I can think of no other dancer of such stature who could accomplish this. Then Fonteyn is a true musician and her training at Sadler's Wells and her contacts with Lambert, Ashton and de Valois have developed this inborn gift.

The ballerina has authority, a kind of arrogance, a gentle gracious arrogance but a quality nevertheless that leaves the audience in no doubt from the moment that she walks on to the stage that she is in full command.

Margot Fonteyn is more than a ballerina, she is *prima ballerina assoluta*, a term that one can only compare to generalissimo.

MARGOT FONTEYN in *Ballet Imperial*, choreography by Balanchine, music Tschaikowsky's second piano concerto, décor and
costumes by Eugene Berman. A beautiful and exciting ballet it had
a triumphant first performance in England at Covent Garden on
April 5th, 1950. This photograph, showing a lovely grande jetée by
Margot Fonteyn, was taken on the stage at Covent Garden against
the front curtain, on the first night.

(*Opposite*) MOIRA SHEARER in *Cinderella* Act III

SHEARER

MOIRA SHEARER in *Les Sylphides* and overleaf in *Cinderella*
and *Les Patineurs*

Moira Shearer has been the victim, and I use the word deliberately, of so much publicity as a result of her role in the novelette-film *Red Shoes* that it becomes difficult to assess her work. She has great and unusual beauty, extraordinary ease and lightness and the unmistakable ' allure ' of a star. All her roles are intelligently conceived, though at times she fails to move one. Only time will show whether a gifted première danseuse will become a prima ballerina.

Few dancers could have resisted more strenuously the allurements and the fierce publicity of the films and have shown a greater sense of values. It is a moot point whether her film experience has helped or retarded her career as a dancer. To me it seems that it will have helped her since it has made her realise how strong is her love of ballet and how nothing must interfere with her progress as a dancer.

MOIRA SHEARER as Cinderella Act I and opposite in Act III

PAMELA MAY as the Fairy Godmother in *Cinderella*

Pamela May was one of the first Wells dancers to emerge and at a difficult time when it was distinctly unfashionable to be British. Her outstanding performances have been as Swanilda in *Coppelia*, the Blue Bird in *The Sleeping Beauty* and in the Ashton-Lambert *Horoscope*. In line and technique Pamela May is one of the purest classical dancers turned out by Sadler's Wells. She has shown great versatility as Baron's camera reveals, but it is as a soubrette that she excels.

(*Left*) MOIRA SHEARER as Cinderella Act I

(*Opposite*) PAMELA MAY in *Nocturne*, choreography Frederick Ashton, décors Sophie Fedorovitch. Music Delius (*Paris*).

PAMELA MAY as The Black Queen in *Checkmate*, choreography Ninette de Valois, costumes and scenery by McKnight Kauffer, and music specially composed by Arthur Bliss.

GREY

Beryl Grey, a dancer with an easy classical technique, a magnificent line and great warmth. She made her debut as a première danseuse during the war when, at a very early age she was entrusted with many leading roles both in the classical and modern repertoires. Her height, unusual for a dancer, has been an undoubted handicap, especially in finding partners, but she makes fine use of it, filling out the musical phrase. Beryl Grey has a wide range ; *Giselle*, both title role and Queen of the Wilis, *The Sleeping Beauty*, both Aurora and the Lilac Fairy, *Swan Lake*. Her finest performance to date perhaps, is in *Ballet Imperial*.

On this page she is seen, from the top left in *Lac des Cygnes*, *Giselle*, Act II, *Lac des Cygnes*, *Carmen* (the opera), *Lac des Cygnes*, Act III, *Sylphides*, *Giselle*, Act I.

BERYL GREY in *Scènes de Ballet*. Choreography Frederick Ashton, music
Igor Stravinsky, costumes and scenery André Beaurepaire.

BERYL GREY in *Giselle*

ELVIN

VIOLETTA ELVIN (formerly Prokhorova) shown here as *Cinderella* came to this country from the Soviet Ballet in which school she received her training. She has danced many of the leading roles at Covent Garden, both the classics and the modern works. She is a most expressive dancer with beautiful arm movements. Her Odette-Odile in *Swan Lake* is especially notable.

FARRON

JULIA FARRON started her career at Sadler's Wells as a classical dancer and then changed to demi-caractère and character roles which she interprets with great intelligence. She is seen here as The Prostitute in *Miracle in the Gorbals*. Her first outstanding demi-caractère performance was in the very difficult small role of Estrella in *Carnaval*, a ballet that is fast disappearing through the necessity of a period interpretation understood today by few dancers. It is a measure of Farron's ability to have brought new life to this creation.

(*Left*) VIOLETTA ELVIN as The Blue Bird in *The Sleeping Beauty*

ANNE HEATON. This young artist was the principal dancer in the Sadler's Wells Theatre Ballet when it was started in 1947. In addition to roles in the classical repertoire she created parts in *Khadra* and *Mardi Gras*. She joined the Covent Garden Company in 1949.

She is seen here in *Les Sylphides*. She is representative of the second generation of English dancer formed by the school and the Sadler's Wells Theatre Ballet which has given opportunities of development to young dancers who might easily have remained in the background had they made their debuts in the major company. This second company, which has already given us Anne Heaton and Nadia Nerina has the same standards and ideals as the first, but the accent is on youth and experiment.

ANNE HEATON in *Khadra*.   Ballet by Celia Franca, music Sibelius (Belshazzar's Feast)
décor and costumes by Honor Frost.   Sadler's Wells Theatre Ballet repertoire.   105

NERINA NADIA NERINA, a South African, who was a leading dancer in the
Sadler's Wells Theatre Ballet before she joined the Covent Garden Company in 1949,
created the Spring Variation in *Cinderella* and has danced the can-can in *La Boutique*
Fantasque, in which role she is shown here

CLAYDON PAULINE CLAYDON first made herself remarked as the Suicide in *Miracle in the Gorbals*, a dramatic performance of real quality, and though not a strong technician from a classical point of view, that same quality informs all her work. She is seen above as Ophelia in Robert Helpmann's *Hamlet*.

LARSEN GERD LARSEN, a beautiful Scandinavian, came to this country shortly after the war and has been dancing leading roles with the Sadler's Wells Ballet, notably The Fairy of the Crystal Fountain in *The Sleeping Beauty*, where her charm is seen to great advantage.

HELPMANN

ROBERT HELPMANN — Dancer — Actor — Choreographer —
Radio Artist, seen here as Albrecht in *Giselle*.

Came from Australia to join the Sadler's Wells Ballet and has
filled every type of role from the classical fairy tale Prince in *The
Sleeping Beauty* to the Fairy Carabosse in the same ballet, from
Giselle's Albrecht to Doctor Coppelius. One cannot capture a
chameleon in a caption, there should be an encyclopaedia of
Helpmann roles and it would be a substantial volume.

Though Robert Helpmann dances the great classical roles it is as a character actor that he excels. His very success as a classical dancer lies in the conviction that he can bring to those princely parts that have with constant repetition become a formula. Helpmann is essentially a man of the theatre in the broadest sense of the term. It was natural therefore when he became a choreographer that he should turn to choreographic drama. This is a dangerous medium in which there have been many failures through the presentation of wordless drama, due

ROBERT HELP-MANN *as the Christ-like visitor to the Gorbals in his own ballet, ' Miracle in the Gorbals' ; a series of pictures showing the serenity of his first appearance and the final agony as he is betrayed and murdered.*

to a misunderstanding of the medium. The narrative must be made clear through the movements and these must depend on the music. As a choreographer Helpmann has combined the actor and the dancer in him.

His first venture *Comus* was a modification of the historic Masque form drawn from Milton's Masque of Comus with music by Purcell, arranged by Lambert and costumes and décors by Oliver Messel. He retains two of Milton's speeches, reciting them magnificently. The work stands so long as Helpmann is cast as Comus.

'*The Rake's Progress*', *the final scene of madness*

In *Hamlet* Helpmann gave a visual commentary based on the lines " For in that sleep of death what dreams may come." He was in fact showing us Hamlet's dying delirium and using for it the only possible medium. It may be claimed that to make the action clear it is necessary to know something of the play and that such a presumption is a weakness. However, in practice as distinct from theory Helpmann cannot be taken to task for flattering the ballet audience. Especially interesting in this ballet is the role of Hurry's décor, as a bridge between Tchaikowsky's romanticism and Helpmann's modern interpretation.

In *Miracle in the Gorbals*, decorated by Edward Burra, the choreographer had for the first time the close collaboration of a composer, Arthur Bliss. This ballet has therefore a magnificent completeness. Helpmann, through his librettist, Michael Benthall, conceives the return of the Master to a squalid Glasgow slum and the inevitable result of his fresh betrayal. This slum and its inhabitants are immediately established both in motion and music. The characters come active as they rarely do in ballet, ' in the round ' and no verbal explanation is necessary at any stage.

Once again some critics were tempted to ask the inevitable ' Is this Ballet ? ' The answer must be very definitely yes. Although the subject is daring and modern there is no essential difference in the relationship between music, dancing, drama and décor than in the case of the first great contemporary dance-drama of *Petrouchka*. Moreover, *Miracle in the Gorbals* could only be danced by a company trained in the classical ballet tradition.

Helpmann's next work, *Adam Zero* (pictured on pages 73, 74 and 75) also had the collaboration of Arthur Bliss and Michael Benthall. Its scenery and costumes are by Roger Furse. It was a magnificent production in which Helpmann himself and June Brae excelled. But symbolism of this cosmic kind is dangerous to handle being either obscure or over obvious.

(*Opposite*) ROBERT HELPMANN as The Stranger in *Miracle in the Gorbals*

The Rake

TURNER

HAROLD TURNER was the first male dancer to establish himself in the new English Ballet. He was trained by Marie Rambert with whom he appeared at the Ballet Club and he partnered Tamara Karsavina in *Le Spectre de la Rose* at The Arts Theatre. Turner has tremendous virility and a strong musical sense, that has enabled him to shine in such roles as the Cancan from *La Boutique Fantasque*, shown above, and as The Miller in *The Three Cornered Hat*, no easy task in succession to Massine, as well as in his own many creations. This combination of athletics and musicality is what our ballet requires.

Overleaf he is seen as Satan in Ninette de Valois' *Job*.

RASSINE

ALEXIS RASSINE, *The Blue Bird*

English male dancers have suffered a serious handicap during the war years and even now military service cuts into a short career. The English dancer is also handicapped by the lack of a tradition either in ballet or folk dancing. This has tended to give the English dancer something of an inferiority complex that success and encouragement could soon dispel, as was seen during the American visit of 1949.

ALEXIS RASSINE in *Les Sylphides*

Alexis Rassine, a South African of Russian parentage is beautifully built for the classic dance and though he tends to be an uneven partner at his best he can dance admirably.(*Overleaf.*) John Hart has great versatility and is developing into an excellent partner, while Michael Somes is the ideal Prince Charming of the ballet, a partner of gallantry and reliability who can always be trusted to give a good performance in both classical and modern roles.

HART

118

JOHN HART in *Scènes de Ballet*

SOMES

(*Right*) MICHAEL SOMES in *Symphonic Variati*

119

GORE

WALTER GORE as Mr. Punch

Walter Gore has been the mainstay of the Ballet Rambert both as choreographer and dancer. He is a virile character dancer—he created the Rake at Sadler's Wells where he was for a time—and his dancing gives the impression of great sincerity. His partnership with Sally Gilmour was especially successful. While *Mr. Punch* was not altogether successful as a ballet its leading role showed Gore at his best. His *Simple Symphony* to the music of Benjamin Britten is both gay and simple and bears repeated visits.

(*Left*) MICHAEL SOMES in *Symphonic Variations*

SALLY GILMOUR and **WALTER GORE** in *Mr. Punch*
Sally Gilmour is a dancer of very great artistry who excels in demi-caractère since she lacks the authority and technique for the classics. She has added two unforgettable portraits to ballet's gallery in the Andrée Howard, David Garnett ballets; Mrs. Tebrick, the vixen woman in *Lady into Fox* and Tulip, the coloured wife in *The Sailor's Return*. The gentle humour and then the pathos that she so subtly conveys make these 'characters in the round'.

GILMOUR

SALLY GILMOUR as Tulip in *The Sailor's Return*

123

BERIOSOVA

124   SVETLANA BERIOSOVA, a young Russian dancer of great promise who led the Metropolitan Ballet, dancing classics and creations, seen above in *Fanciulla delle Rose*.

BALLET THEATRE
Birth of an American Tradition

Lucia Chase's Ballet Theatre that came to Covent Garden in 1946 brought us the native American ballet that had grown up, as did our ballet, under Russian influence. Its programme was made up of the familiar Russian repertoire, the works of Antony Tudor, and typically American ballets, notably by Jerome Robbins, Agnes de Mille and William Dollar. The first were done conscientiously, but a conscientious performance of *Petrouchka* has no real meaning. The most ambitious and successful work was Antony Tudor's *Pillar of Fire*, of which *Jardin au Lilas* was a foretaste. It introduced a magnificent tragédienne in Nora Kaye. The American, *Fancy Free, Interplay* and *On Stage*, were in an idiom familiar to film fans but so superbly interpreted by classically trained dancers that they appeared as something new. The vitality of these young Americans and their physical beauty carried all before it. A few asked ' but is it ballet ? ' They ask it with every work that has no classical variations or adagios. Of course it is ballet ; American ballet ; and the beginning of a new form of an art that has travelled from Versailles to Italy, St. Petersburg, London and New York continually enriching itself.

Interplay by Jerome Robbins, music by Morton Gould
This is a danced interpretation of the music, a remarkable piece of craftsmanship in which classicism and the modern idiom meet, giving us beauty, wit, satire, humour and a pinch of vulgarity. *All the pictures in this section were taken on stage at Covent Garden in the summer of 1946.*

126

) *Fancy Free* (Jerome
bins), music by Bern-
, décor and costumes
r Smith. An American
on of *Les Matelots*, the
old theme of three
rs on leave, superbly
ed by JEROME ROB-
, MICHAEL KIDD
JOHN KRIZA.

) Scenes from Michael
's *On Stage*, music by
Joio, décor and cos-
s by Oliver Smith and
ael Kidd.

nventional peep back-
, ingeniously produced
made noteworthy by
's own Chaplinesque
(*Right*) MICHAEL
and ALICIA
NSO.

127

Pillar of Fire. One of the most moving dances in all modern ballet. NORA KAYE and HUGH LAING

NORA KAYE in *Pillar of Fire*
On next two pages scenes from *Pillar of Fire*

Pillar of Fire firmly established the reputation of Antony Tudor in America.
It is a drama of small town life in New England, it has been called a psychological
ballet but that is misleading since it implies something involved.   The characterisation is crystal clear from the moment that the curtain rises on the love-starved
Hagar, so magnificently danced by Nora Kaye.   Tudor has adapted the classical
technique to discipline his very alert observation of natural movement and the
dancing flows directly from the music of Schoenberg's *Verklarte Nacht*.   Jo
Mielziner's settings and costumes establish the atmosphere.

NORA KAYE is pictured here in the Pas de Deux with the choreographer
ANTONY TUDOR himself.   (*Right*) NORA KAYE in *Pillar of Fire*.

NORA KAYE AND HUGH LAING

Jardin au Lilas

This ballet was first produced for Marie Rambert's company at the Mercury Theatre and afterwards taken over by Ballet Theatre. Today it is in both repertoires. Set to the music of Chausson it succeeds admirably in suggesting an undercurrent of drama and mystery without ever underlining it. The dancing is fluid, a rich pattern of exits and entrances. If *Pillar of Fire* is a novel then this is a short story by the same hand, an episode in a lilac drenched Park. What is extraordinary is the completely French atmosphere suggested by this young Englishman.

Jardin au Lilas. NORA KAYE and HUGH LAING

ALICIA ALONSO AND ANTONY TUDOR
Choreography by Antony Tudor, music by Chausson, décor and costumes by
Raymond Sovey after Hugh Stevenson.

ALICIA ALONSO in *Waltz Academy*
Ballet by Balanchine, music Rieti, décor and costumes Smith and Colt.

Gala Performance

This ballet by Antony Tudor sets out to caricature the balletic styles of France, Italy and Russia. Its keynote should be wit, it should be subtle, penetrating, revealing. Instead it treats us to a display of knock-about humour, and egged on by the audience its interpreters usually forget themselves in their efforts to raise an extra laugh.

(*Top p.* 138) NORA KAYE as the Russian Ballerina, ALICIA ALONSO the Italian, NORMAN VASLAVINA the French. (*Below p.* 138) ANTONY TUDOR, NORA KAYE, ALICIA ALONSO, NORMAN VASLAVINA and HUGH LAING.

138

Romeo and Juliet

In *Romeo and Juliet* Antony Tudor has attempted the impossible, the telling of Shakespeare's play without words. Moreover, he has had the additional handicap of Delius' music for *A Village Romeo and Juliet*. Had he, like Helpmann with *Hamlet*, given a visual interpretation of an aspect of the story and refrained from attempting to show it in detail he might have succeeded. If the ballet fails as a whole, as it must do, it has scenes of very great beauty such as the robing of Juliet for her marriage which live on their own. The costumes and settings of Eugene Berman and the dancing of Nora Kaye and Hugh Laing were outstanding, so outstanding indeed that they made one long for the words, as one might in a television play when the sound has been cut off.

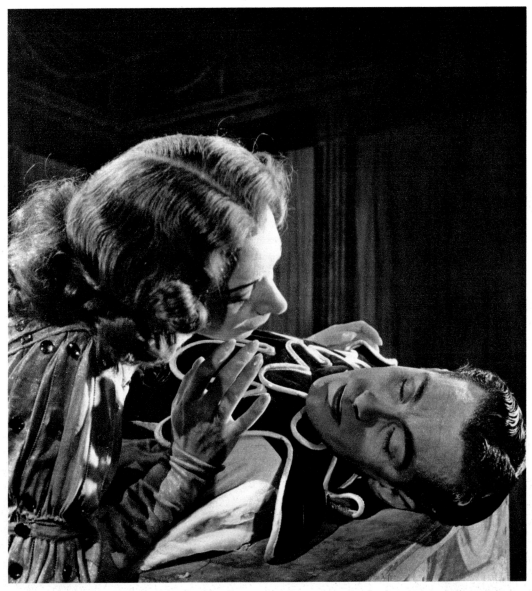

NORA KAYE and HUGH LAING in *Romeo and Juliet*

Romeo and Juliet. The Balcony Scene. HUGH LAING and NORA KAYE

Romeo and Juliet. NORA KAYE and HUGH LAING

Undertow

A ballet by Antony Tudor on a theme by Van Druten, music Schumann, décor and costumes, Raymond Bremin.

In *Jardin au Lilas* and *Pillar of Fire* Antony Tudor was always complete master of his theme which he translated perfectly into terms of the dance. The same has been the case in the very grim themes selected by Roland Petit in *Le Jeune Homme et la Mort* and *Carmen*. In *Undertow* the theme is sordid and because it is not translated into ballet the result is displeasing. More is attempted here than is possible in ballet. The dancers Diana Adams and John Kriza showed a classical school that won immediate favour with English audiences grounded in the classics. From the first night of their appearance Diana Adams was hailed as the American Beryl Grey.

Undertow
DIANA ADAMS—JOHN KRIZA—HUGH LAING

DIANA ADAMS and HUGH LAING in *Undertow*

MICHAEL KIDD as *Petrouchka*

Although Michael Kidd gave a sensitive performance this ballet is
as Russian as *Fancy Free* is American.   *Petrouchka* lives when its
crowd can think as Russians and even the later Russian companies
who filled the fair ground with non-Russian supers failed to bring the
drama to life.

(*Opposite*) RAM GOPAL as The Eag

NOUVEAUX BALLETS DE MONTE CARLO
(Cambridge Theatre)

This company, assembled and controlled by Serge Lifar, introduced some outstanding personalities to London. That was its major weakness, there were so many stars that there was no company. The choreography apart from *Giselle* and some Diaghileff revivals was by Serge Lifar and was not presented with the care and proper art direction it receives at the Opéra. The dancers it brought to London were Yvette Chauviré, Janine Charrat, Ludmilla Tcherina, Renée Jeanmaire, Sirène Adjemova, Olga Adabache, Vladimir Skouratoff and Alexandre Kalioujny. The main creation was Lifar's *Chota Roustaveli*, 1947, a four act, three hour work based on a Georgian theme. It had moments of great poetic beauty and much invention, but it needed pruning, a proper scenic setting and a fully disciplined corps de ballet.

YVETTE CHAUVIRE in *Chota Roustaveli*
Taken on stage at Cambridge Theatre in 1946.

145

ALEXANDRE KALIOUJNY in *Prince Igor*, the most inspiring performance seen for a very long time. He is today a premier danseur étoile of the Opéra, Paris, belongs to the same class of dancer as Adolf Bolm, Leon Woizikowski, Yura Lazovsky, Shabelevsky and those other Polovtsian warriors who made the conquest of Western Europe in 1909. He is a Slav dancer par excellence and in his *Prince Igor* he brings back a whole period that is very far away from us today. But in addition to his character work he is versatile and well built enough to acquit himself really well in the classics, notably *The Blue Bird*.

LUDMILLA TCHERINA and EMILE AUDRAN in *Mephisto Valse*, ballet by Lifar, music by Liszt.

148

Ballet Duets

Modern ballet conditions with the great difficulty of large travelling companies have developed the two person ballet as something quite distinct from pas de deux seized from its context and placed in the middle of a programme. Previously the most famous, indeed the only self contained work of this type, that comes to mind was *Le Spectre de la Rose*, first produced in 1911. The essence of this two person ballet is that it should be complete in itself, indeed it has much the same relationship to the large ballet as the sonnet to the epic poem.

Ballet of this type places an enormous burden on the dancers, both from the point of view of endurance and of sustained interpretation, especially when one remembers that the longest adagio in classical ballet lasts about five minutes, and the average variation under two. These two person ballets have been especially developed by Serge Lifar who has been fortunate in having artists who can fully exploit their dramatic possibilities.

Lifar's work has been greatly underestimated both in England and America. He has recreated the French school and his work has for the first time in France given the choreographer a status generally recognised by other artists. Levinson devoted his last volume to Lifar, and Lifar's *Pensées sur la Danse* was prefaced by Paul Valéry and illustrated by Maillol. He is a major personality.

Pictured here and on p. 150 are COLETTE MARCHAND and SERGE PERRAULT in *Romeo and Juliet*, which Serge Lifar has based on Tchaikowsky's symphonic poem. This work has moments of great beauty and at the same time passages where it is quite impossible for two characters to match the volume and intensity of the music.

LES BALLETS DES CHAMPS ELYSEES

Paris has long been a spiritual centre of ballet creation as distinct from dancing, and the Champs Elysées are in the heart of Paris. *Les Ballets des Champs Elysées*, under the leadership of Boris Kochno and Roland Petit came into being in 1945 and had their headquarters at the inspired and inspiring Théatre de Champs Elysées, created, as wrote Gabriel Astrue, " pour la gloire de Bourdelle et de Claude Debussy."

This young company—and the accent is on youth—can well be called the shock troops of modern ballet. They made a great impact in London when they arrived shortly after the war. England had been starved of foreign visitors for so long; they were a revelation.

The majority of the works were by Roland Petit—it seems difficult to realise that this very young man was even then a major force in French Ballet, and the company had assembled such artists as Wakhevitch, Bérard and Malclés, once again reminding us that the painter, as well as the poet has always played an important role in French Ballet.

The company's creations were all new to London, with the exception of the few classical pas de deux incorporated into the programmes, not always happily it is true, but valuable if only to remind us that although variety, novelty and constant creation was the theme of the company, classicism still played its part. Apart from *Les Forains*, *Jeux de Cartes*, *La Sylphide* and *Le Jeune Homme et la Mort*, already described at some length in this book, the company has shown us such works as *Le Rendezvous*, with Brassai's photographic background against which " deux enfants amoureux s'embrassent dans la nuit " oblivious of the tragedy of the Paris streets that is unfolded with all the realism and fantasy of the modern French film; the bitter sweet *Treize Danses* in which Grétry and Verlaine happily wedded dance in the setting of Dior; *Création*, a choreographic essay by David Lichine without music or décor, showing the mind of the choreographer at work; *Les Amours de Jupiter*, and the acrobatic masterpiece, *Oedipus and the Sphinx*. Aurel Milloss, well known for his work in Italy, has created a ballet on the company—*The Portrait of Don Quixote*, thus underlining the international outlook of this most French of companies. Janine Charrat, France's other young choreographer, first found herself in this company.

Boris Kochno, like Diaghileff, has unlimited faith in youth and would rather present the passionate experiments of young people than the proved works of the old master.

JEAN BABILEE is the outstanding dancer of today, whether in the modern *Le Jeune Homme et la Mort* or the classical *Blue Bird*. He is musical, an actor with his whole body and a formidable athlete. His leaps thrill one by their seeming recklessness and enchant by the quality of their plastique. Yet there is always something that escapes, a touch of genius that cannot be listed. He started at the Opéra and during the occupation joined Marika Besobrasova's company at Cannes. He was an original member of Les Ballets des Champs Elysées and has made his career in this company. His greatest roles have been The Jester in *Jeux de Cartes*, so well depicted here, the hunchback in *Le Rendezvous*, *Le Jeune Homme et la Mort*, Don Quixote in *La Portrait de Don Quixote* and in his own *L'Amour et son Amour*, a first work that was wonderfully musical and refreshingly simple. His partnership with his wife, Nathalie Phillipart has been outstanding.

BORIS KOCHNO

151

152

JEAN BABILEE as The Jester in *Jeux de Cartes*

Jeux de Cartes

Jeux de Cartes is set to the difficult music of Stravinsky and its creator, then aged 21, was the pathetic scrap of a child who danced and acted in *La Mort du Cygne.* Its theme tells of the changing fortunes in a game of poker where the joker is running wild. From the point of view of its musical treatment and its pattern this is a very remarkable achievement, it is difficult to imagine that it is the work of a very young girl. Also she has given a magnificent role to a male dancer, Jean Babilée. He gives excitement in a ballet that is by no means always dramatically clear. (*Jean Babilée as the Jester on this page.*) Pierre Roy's setting and costumes are in the best French tradition. He brings us right into the arena as if we were looking over the players and on to the table. It is in the collaboration of painter and choreographer that French ballet excels and for this reason French ballets have served as such fine subjects for the photographer. The photographs really do render the flavour of the ballet.

154

Les Forains

ROLAND PETIT'S *Les Forains* is a very great minor work, one of those artist's sketches that suggest so much by leaving so much unsaid. Here are the circus folk, straight out of a Picasso blue period canvas. They set up their booth, limber up and put on their tattered finery. The small crowd gathers and the performance begins. And with the excitement of the performance these poor wanderers are transformed. They give of their very best. But when the hat comes round the crowd melts away. Suddenly they are very tired. They pack their belongings on to their handcart and dismantle the booth. They take the road again. But the little girl has forgotten her dove and just as the curtain falls she runs across the stage to retrieve it.

This ballet has a number of delightfully conceived dances, perfect translations of the circus just as Sauguet's brilliant score is a perfect translation of circus music, it also has the atmosphere of sadness that is always in the background even when the gaiety is at its height. Christian Bérard, a genius of the theatre, has given it costumes and a setting that are a part of the choreography, not only in feeling but in fact since the set is assembled and dismantled by the characters.

Les Forains. ROLAND PETIT, SOLANGE, SCHWARZ, SIMONE MOSTOVOY and TEDDY RODOLPHE *Taken on stage at The Adelphi Theatre in 1946*

Les Forains.　A group that suggests a blue period Picasso
SOLANGE SCHWARZ—ROLAND PETIT—SIMONE MOSTOVOY AND
TEDDY RODOLPHE

DANIELLE DARMANCE

In the type of ballet conceived by Boris Kochno the idea comes first and then the dancers must be found who will best illustrate it. Inspiration may be found at the cabaret or circus—did not Diaghileff himself find a passage in one of his ballets for the talented busker who played spoons to the queue outside the Alhambra? One of the most interesting importations into ballet has been Danielle Darmance, a cabaret dancer of very great elegance. Often a classical dancer takes easily to cabaret work, but here is a cabaret artist who has taken to classical ballet, and the result is cabaret with a classical plastique.

She has been seen to great effect in *Le Bal des Blanchisseuses*—pictured here, and *Treize Danses*.

Le Bal des Blanchisseuses, by Roland Petit with music by Vernon Duke, the former Vladimir Dukelsky, and scenery and costumes by Stanislas Lepri is a very lightweight frolic whose only distinction is Lepri's brilliant décors, variations on hanging up the washing, and Darmance's acrobatics. Roland Petit shows in this ballet and in the later *Oeuf a la Coq* a nostalgia for the musical comedy stage and an undoubted brilliance in handling such work. It is however out of place in ballet because it is badly organised, a series of startling improvisations not closely related to the music or consistent in style. It would be equally out of place in the new type of musical that requires consistency and tautness, but both *Bal des Blanchisseuses* and *Oeuf a la Coq* are rich in material.

La Sylphide

La Sylphide, music by Schneitzhoffer, produced in 1830, conquered the ballet for romanticism, established the fame of Taglioni, paved the way for Pavlova, Spessivtseva, Markova and is still with us in Les Sylphides, that borrowed its name and retained its essence. *La Sylphide* brought with it miles of white tarlatan, raised the ballerina *sur les pointes* and sent the male dancer to a long and humiliating banishment.

Now with the help of Victor Gsovsky, Christian Bérard's restatement of the décors and the romantic lithographs Boris Kochno has revived it, restated would be more accurate, for Les Ballets des Champs Elysées. Characteristically Kochno has found his own classic, has made a novelty from a period piece.

In Nina Vyroubova, now danseuse étoile of the opera, he has found his ideal sylphide. " Elle était si pale, elle était si chaste et si triste ", as Jules Janin wrote of Taglioni. One can only continue the quotation : " Mais personne ne saurait dire combien de douleurs mademoiselle Taglioni savait mettre dans le dénouement de son drame : on eut dit l'agonie d'un beau lis ; elle mourait peu à peu, lentement, d'une mort aérienne . . . "

La Sylphide. Act. II. NINA VYROUBOVA and ROLAND PETIT

NINA VYROUBOVA and ROLAND PETIT in *La Sylphide* Act II
VYROUBOVA established her reputation in London by three performances of this ballet
at the Winter Garden Theatre in 1948. (Overleaf, p. 160 VYROUBOVA in *La Sylphide*
Act II, p. 161 Vyroubova with HELENE SADOVSKA in *La Sylphide* Act II)

Les Amours de Jupiter, choreography Roland Petit, music Jacques Ibert, costumes and décors Jean Hugo is based on Ovid's *Metamorphoses* and deals with Jupiter's amours on his visits to the earth. We see him as the Bull with Europa, the Swan with Leda, we feel his presence when he comes to Danae as the golden rain and then in the guise of an eagle he carries off the shepherd Ganymede. Finally he returns to Juno to whom he has always been true, ' in his fashion '.

This is a difficult subject in which much more must be suggested than is shown. Petit has found the perfect stylisation that retains the classical feeling yet presents it in modern form. This is a success that parallels Giraudoux' *Amphitrion* '38. It is the most erotic ballet I have seen on the stage, far more so than the same choreographer's *Carmen*, but nowhere has he offended, so sure and delicate has been his touch.

BALLET RAMBERT

MARIE RAMBERT was born in Poland, and was a pupil of the great Jacques Dalcroze, inventor of the system of Eurhythmics. When Diaghileff asked Dalcroze to send him a teacher to assist Nijinsky in his choreographic education Marie Rambert was his choice, and once in the entourage of the Russian Ballet she became an enthusiastic convert.

At the end of the first world war she started a ballet school in Ladbroke Road, the aim of which was to train pupils to take their place in the Diaghileff ballet. Diaghileff in fact earmarked one or two promising candidates when he died in 1929.

Marie Rambert had already produced a small ballet, *The Tragedy of Fashion*, with choreography by an unknown young man, Frederick Ashton, and this ballet was so successful

that it was later included in *Riverside Nights* at the Lyric, Hammersmith. It was the first Rambert Ballet and in fact the first English ballet under the new tradition. When Diaghileff died Marie Rambert had to find an outlet for the talent in her studio and in 1930 she started the Ballet Club at the Mercury and gave her little company a permanent headquarters. It was here on the tiny stage, that " chamber ballet " as it came to be known, was born with a whole series of delightful vignettes by Ashton, Andrée Howard and others.

Her little group contributed largely to the existence of the Camargo Society, the start of British Ballet. She can rightly be called one of the founders of British Ballet. She has always had an eye for talent and she added to her little group such choreographers as Antony Tudor and Frank Staff, while apart from the beautiful Pearl Argyle, Prudence Hyman, Diana Gould, Maude Lloyd, William Chappell and Harold Turner, she numbered among her dancers Sally Gilmour and Walter Gore, both of whom are discussed elsewhere in this book. The creations of the Ballet Rambert are so widely known as to need no introduction : *Lady into Fox*, *Mr. Punch*, *Simple Symphony*, *Dark Elegies*, *The Sailor's Return*, to mention but a few.

As the popularity of ballet grew and larger companies appeared the Ballet Rambert found itself artistically cramped without the revenue to expand. In 1947 she bravely took her little company to Australia and New Zealand where for over a year she played to capacity. She left behind a heritage that is developing into a state subsidised Australian Ballet. Wherever Marie Rambert goes she has been the inspiration upon which others have built, making names for themselves which are now household words in the ballet world.

164   ELIZABETH SCHOOLING in *Bar aux Folies Bergères*

The Sailor's Return

First produced on June 2nd 1947 with choreography, décor and costumes by Andrée Howard and specially composed score by Arthur Oldham.

Photographed here are SALLY GILMOUR as Tulip — the coloured wife — and WALTER GORE as The Sailor.

The Sailor (WALTER GORE) falls in love with Tulip (SALLY GILMOUR). *Taken on the stage at Sadler's Wells Theatre 1947.*

165

The Sailor's Return

ANDREE HOWARD was one of Marie Rambert's first choreographers in the heroic days of the Ballet Club. She is sensitive, musical and a good decorative artist. Though she has created many works for the Sadler's Wells Theatre Ballet, all of them interesting, it is on a smaller scale that she is most successful. Her outstanding works are *Lady into Fox* and *The Sailor's Return* where the concentration is on the personal relationship of a few characters. *Taken on the stage at Sadler's Wells Theatre.*

(Right) ANDREE HOWARD

166

RETURN OF ORIGINAL BALLETS RUSSES

To the new generation of balletomanes the name of Colonel de Basil's Original Ballets Russes, with or without the addition of Monte Carlo, had the same magic that the name of Diaghileff's had to their fathers. In 1947 de Basil was back at Covent Garden. For a number of reasons the spell was broken. In the ten years interval we had seen the style and homogeneity of our own Ballet and the exciting novelties that the French and Americans had brought us. The Russian company, much battered by its war wanderings, was hastily assembled for the season and in any case only a handful of Russians remained. The old ballets had lost their sharpness; *Le Beau Danube* was a badly repainted fresco, *Schéhérazade* no longer thrilled, the *Polovtsian Dances* were tamed by the smiling showgirls who had taken the place of the savage maidens, and *Les Présages* had lost its pattern. Those with memories felt thwarted, the youngsters could not imagine what all the fuss had been about.

DE BASIL AND HASKELL

One charming novelty pleased the audience, *Graduation Ball*. Produced by David Lichine in Australia at the beginning of the war. It was gay and lighthearted, it was danced to an admirable arrangement of Strauss melodies by Antal Dorati. Many critics found it too American for Russian Ballet but since its conception and setting were by Alexandre Benois this seems a little far fetched. *Graduation Ball* reintroduced Riabouchinska and Lichine to the public and also the sparkling Renée Jeanmaire, who had been seen at the Cambridge Theatre with Serge Lifar. Jeanmaire was largely miscast, especially in *Les Sylphides*, on the opening night, but made a strong impression in *Le Fils Prodigue* and in *Piccoli*, a novelty by Boris Kniaseff that was given three performances.

Backstage
M. LARIONOV and an assistant discussing a prop with DAVID LICHINE.

RIABOUCHINSKA and LICHINE in a rehearsal of *Graduation Ball* with Charwomen in attendance, an unconscious ballet seized upon by Baron who has an eye for 'news' as well as ballet. This remarkable chance composition was not posed.

LICHINE and RIABOUCHINSKA

Both these dancers were among the original de Basil 'babies', Monte Carlo, 1932, and both have been trained in the studio of Kchessinska.

Riabouchinska has made a number of roles her own; Frivolity in *Les Présages*, the good pupil in *Schola di ballo*, the young girl in *Le Beau Danube*, the child in *Jeux d'Enfants*, Cinderella in Fokline's ballet, the cock in *Coq d'Or* and especially the maiden in *Paganini*. Her strength has lain in these demi-caractère creations which have coloured the whole of Russian Ballet from 1932-1939. Her most noteworthy role in the repertoire ballet has been the prelude in *Les Sylphides*.

Lichine, a dancer of tremendous vitality whose Passion in *Les Présages* was his outstanding role has danced but little of recent years and has concentrated on choreography showing great inventiveness though often going astray in the planning of a work.

BORIS KNIASEFF

Boris Kniaseff has played a very large role, especially in France as an inspiring teacher of the classical dance. Yvette Chauviré and Renée Jeanmaire in particular owe a great deal to his tuition. He has done choreography for many ballets, only *Piccoli* and *Biroska* having been seen in England. His not very fortunate use of already existing music has been a serious flaw in judging them as a whole.

169

Piccoli VLADIMIR DOKOUDOUSKY, in *Piccoli*, pupil of Preobrajenska, who became a premier danseur with de Basil during the war and attracted great attention by his virility and his excellent comic mime.

RENÉE JEANMAIRE in *Piccoli*

Graduation Ball

(*Above*) NICHOLAS ORLOFF as The Drummer in the most striking solo number in *Graduation Ball*.

(*Opposite*) The Cadets led by LICHINE, salute the young girls and invite them to dance. (*Below*) RIABOUCHINSKA and LICHINE lead the *Graduation Ball*. *Taken on the stage at Covent Garden in 1947.*

LICHINE and RIABOUCHINSKA in *Graduation Ball*

(*Opposite*) TAMARA TOUMANOVA in *Don Qui*

A GALLERY OF INTERNATIONAL PORTRAITS

TOUMANOVA

TAMARA TOUMANOVA in *Swan Lake*

TOUMANOVA, the original baby ballerina—she danced a leading role at the Opéra at the age of eleven—was first seen in London at the Savoy in *Les Ballets* 1933 and afterwards with de Basil until she joined the René Blum company at Drury Lane in 1939. During the war she danced and filmed in America returning to Paris at the Opéra in 1947 and to London with the du Cuevas Ballet in 1949.

She has the grand Russian manner, an exceptionally strong technique and wonderful beauty. Today she is rarely given an opportunity of showing the sensitivity that was so outstanding in such ballets as *Concurrence* and *Cotillon*, but when she subordinates an exciting virtuosity that can come perilously close to acrobatics to interpretation she has few equals as a ballerina.

MASSINE

Leonide Massine, more than any other individual, represents
Diaghileff Ballet. He first came into prominence as a young dan[c]
in 1914 in *Joseph's Legend*. During the war, he began his chore[o]
graphic education, emerging three years later, an undoubted mast[er]
with *Le Tricorne* and *La Boutique Fantasque*. As a dancer, too,
first saw the full extent of his artistry in 1917, and his partnersh[ip]
with Lydia Lopokova became as noteworthy as the partnership [of]
Karsavina and Nijinsky. Massine who has a genius for rhythm a[nd]
style both of period and country, profited by the travels of t[he]
Diaghileff Company in Spain (*Le Tricorne*), in Italy (*Good Humou[red]
Ladies*), and later with works inspired by French thought. He h[as]
enormously enriched the repertoire of movement, translating fo[lk]
dance into ballet, and borrowing much from the modern dan[ce]
Here seen as the Miller in *Three Cornered Hat*; opposite as t[he]
Shoemaker in the film *Red Shoes*.

GOLLNER

NANA GOLLNER,
started her artistic life
Hollywood starlet,
her name in ballet wit
René Blum company
a brief apprenticeship
Colonel de Basil, whor
afterwards rejoined. S
a true classical ball
dignified and authori
with no mannerisms o
cess of virtuosity to
figure her work.

EGLEVSKY

André Eglevsky first attracted attention as a child with the de Basil company—those slow turns in *Les Présages* are still quoted. He has enormous technical ease, such ease that he sometimes gives an impression of nonchalence and the interpretation of his roles suffers. But though Eglevsky is always Eglevsky, it is always a pleasure to see work of such quality and virility.

MARCHAND

COLLETTE MARCHAND, as Agathe, the white cat in *Les Demoiselles de la Nuit*. This role was originally created in Paris by Roland Petit for Margot Fonteyn. The ballet based on a theme by Jean Anouilh, with dresses and décors by Léonor Fini and a witty score by Jean Françaix, tells the story of the love of a poet for a white cat, her transformation into a woman and her relapse on their wedding night when she is summoned on to the roof tops by the Ginger Cat. Petit's choreography with its suggestion of feline movement and his characterisation of the tragic cat-woman make this one of the outstanding post-war creations, complete in choreography, music and décors.

It is interesting to compare this talented French dancer's interpretation of the role with that of Margot Fonteyn. The colour picture frontispiece is of Margot Fonteyn maskless on the roof of the theatre where she first created the role.

JEANMAIRE

Renée Jeanmaire revealed herself but slowly to the British public though from the first her strong classical technique and her intelligence were obvious. She made her London début with Serge Lifar's Monte Carlo Ballet at the Cambridge Theatre 1947. She had until then been at the Opéra where she received her early training. She next appeared at Covent Garden with Col. de Basil's original Ballets Russes. Here she was not seen to very great advantage; *Les Sylphides* was not for her, she lacked the authority for Aurora and the fouetté-turning girl in *Graduation Ball* was too trivial by far. Only in Lichine's *Prodigal Son* could one catch a glimpse of the powerful acting to come in *Carmen* while the three performances of *Piccoli*, based entirely on her personality were a delight. Her next appearance was with a dance-concert group at the Princes Theatre, *Les Etoiles de la Danse*. Here the single piano and the lack of scenery and corps de ballet gave no ambience; the champagne was there but a trifle flat and served in a tooth glass. It was with Roland Petit's Ballets de Paris that we saw the true Jeanmaire, or at any rate one aspect of her personality. It will be a pity if she is never allowed to escape from being a ' femme fatale.'

To describe Jeanmaire it would be far easier to use the French language. She is essentially French in her attack, a Parisienne. There is wit and a fine intelligence prompting every movement.

RENÉE JEANMAIRE in *Carmen*

DANILOVA

Alexandra Danilova has the grand manner. She is the last of those trained in the Imperial schools, and she became the last ballerina of the Diaghileff company, a superb pedigree in an aristocratic art. Her performances in *Swan Lake*, Act II, *Le Beau Danube* and *La Boutique Fantasque* will long remain in the memory and by her example she has inspired Markova, Toumanova, Baronova and all the younger dancers who have been privileged to be in a company with her.

On her return to London in 1949 she danced with Frederic Franklin, an English dancer who made his name in America and who impressed his audiences by his gallant partnering and his fine musical sense. She is seen here as Swanilda in *Coppélia*, Act I.

ALEXANDRA DANILOVA and **FREDERIC FRANKLIN** in *Coppélia* Act II
Taken on the stage at Covent Garden in 1949.

SKIBINE   GEORGE SKIBINE in *Sebastian*.   Choreography by Edward
Caton, music by Gian-Carlo Menotti, décors Oliver Smith, costumes Milena.

MARJORIE TALLCHIEF as the Queen of the Wilis in *Giselle*

TALLCHIEF

Marjorie Tallchief, one of two famous dancing sisters, is a young American dancer who has improved out of all recognition in her seasons with the de Cuevas ballet. She has turned an excess of strength into true dancing and her Queen of the Wilis—ungrateful role—is one of the finest seen for many years. Her dancing in *Concerto Barocco* shows her ability in phrasing.

MARJORIE TALLCHIEF and GEORGE SKIBINE in *Concerto Barocco*, ballet
by Balanchine to the music of Bach (*Concerto in D* for two violins).
(*Opposite*) TATIANA RIABOUCHINSKA in *Le Coq D'Or*

PAGAVA

Ethéry Pagava, Parisian born Georgian dancer, made her London début at the age of 13 with Roland Petit at the Adelphi Theatre as the little girl in *Les Forains*. She fell and broke her arm on the first night. She made her reappearance as a première danseuse with the Grand Ballet de Monte Carlo at Covent Garden in 1948 and made the outstanding hit of the season in George Balanchine's *Warning Shadows*. Only at the beginning of her career, Pagava looks like repeating the success of the famous children of 1933.

GEORGES SKIBINE is a romantic rather than a purely classical dancer and few of the younger generation of male dancers can show his ballerina to greater advantage. Though he can be gallantly self-effacing—and what a quality that is—when necessary he has the dramatic power to make an enormous impact on an audience whose sympathy he has won from the start by his bearing and physique.

Balanchine's *Concerto-Barocco*, together with his *Warning Shadows* was the most outstanding work shown us by the Grand Ballet de Monte Carlo.

Balanchine is a highly trained musician and the visual interpretation of music, especially the music of Bach, is the type of problem in which he excels.

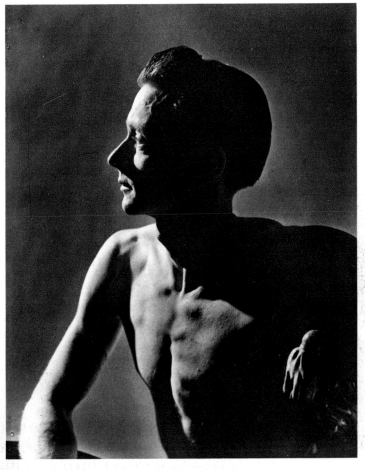

MARJORIE TALLCHIEF as the Queen of the Wilis in *Giselle*

CARMEN

Roland Petit's *Carmen* is no exception to the rule that in France the poet or littérateur occupies a major role in ballet creation. We have seen it in *Giselle* and *Le Jeune Homme et la Mort*. In this case though the writer is dead, it is nevertheless Merimée who dominates and it is Merimée's Carmen that we see rather than Bizet's. The use of Bizet's music for another purpose than that for which it was written is a flaw in the structure of the ballet, especially as the *Habanera* is made into a weak and uninteresting male solo. Once that has been admitted one can only admire the extraordinarily powerful effect of Petit's production.

He has told the familiar story in five episodes. The first is the quarrel outside the cigarette factory and Don José's meeting with Carmen. Don José has been made into a civilian so that while his emotional relationship with Carmen remains substantially unchanged, we are not shown the added conflict between duty and passion. Petit was probably right in tightening and simplifying a story that can only be told in action. This first scene contains little actual dancing but introduces the characters and establishes them through a number of what one might call " production " details as distinct from choreography.

The second scene takes place in the tavern of Lilas Pastia, *sur les ramparts de Séville*. Here there is a true choreographic pattern in a dance that suggests Spain though it is never in the Spanish idiom. In a remarkable dance Carmen is fully established, more fully established than ever in the opera.   In this act Don José, a negative figure as he must be from a dramatic point of view throughout the drama, is guilty of the one choreographic flaw, his solo rendering of the *Habanera* a pseudo-Spanish touch quite out of keeping with the rest.

The next scene shows Carmen's bedroom after his wooing of Carmen. It is realistic, it contains details that might be considered sordid, for instance his wiping his hands on the lace curtain, but this realism has been treated with great skill, it has been completely translated into terms of ballet once the atmosphere has been suggested. Seldom has a choreographer been able to depict characters more in the round ; Don José's pride in his conquest, his weak jealousy, Carmen's completely animal reaction, her desire for fresh sensation, her wish to goad the unfortunate man who has left her incompletely satisfied. The exit of Carmen and the smugglers with the unwilling Don José is a magnificent curtain.

The fourth scene in which the décor with its slowly revolving cartwheels plays a major role, sees Don José inveigled into crime and then deserted. And because of the nightmare composition of the set with its twisted forms and shadows the sense of Don José's solitariness is painfully absolute. He is lost, alone in a prison suggested by the spokes of the wheels and their long shadows.

The final scene is outside the arena. Escamillo is established in a moment as a bombastic posturing hero, a slight distortion of the music that is forgivable for its dramatic effectiveness in this context. Then comes to the sound of drum beats the final duel between Carmen and Don José, an echo of the death struggle that is going on inside the arena. There is the overpowering feeling that though Carmen is stabbed to death, it is Don José who is the real victim. The curtain falls on the ironic note of Escamillo's triumph with a cascade of hats thrown into the air by the aficionados.

Petit's choreography and Clavé's décors are inseparable, Bizet alone remains aloof from the partnership, a magnificent background it is true, but still a background. The interpretation could not be bettered. Jeanmaire *is* Carmen, so completely Carmen, that it will be difficult for her to escape into another role.

It is a moot point how far realism can be carried in such an art of illusion as ballet and *Carmen* certainly reaches the very limits. Has it surpassed them?

I am not thinking here of the subject but of its treatment. Has this material been translated into choreography? Petit first of all conceived *Carmen* in terms of the dance, and Carmen is as full of recognisable dancing as the opera itself is full of melodies that can be hummed. The first act creates an atmosphere, the second has an ensemble dance, the dance of Don José and Carmen's dance, the third is almost entirely made up of a pas de deux, the fourth creates atmosphere, the final act has Escamillo's solo and then the Don José–Carmen pas de deux. The ballet certainly does not lack dances.

Having created his dances Petit's next function, and I saw him at work, was to *produce* the ballet. And it is here that we have the touches of realism, the business with the cigarettes and other details that complete the picture. Such production is entirely legitimate in a narrative ballet so long as it is added and is not of the main structure of the work, so long as it does not come between music and movement. The classic composer allowed for long passages of mime, Bizet in *Carmen* allows for a spoken dialogue in between the arias. In taking advantage of this Petit has understood the music far more thoroughly than those opera producers who try to make *Carmen* into a grand opera and distort it by having the spoken passages sung.

The bedroom pas de deux is daring, it may shock many sensitive people, but that is not the point except for the censor or the moralist. It is definitely translated into a dance, I cannot believe that Don José and Carmen would behave like this in the solitude of their room. A realistic French film producer would soon show us differently. Every pas de deux is a *duo d'amour*, this one deals with passion as the similar one in *Les Desmoiselles de la Nuit* did with tenderness. It is open to discussion whether Petit could have succeeded better in depicting the characters of Carmen and Don José and the situation between them by a more subtle approach. I for one do not believe that he could but I sincerely hope that neither Petit himself nor any other choreographer will again attempt anything so risky. (*Taken at a special photocall for this book at the Prince's Theatre* 1948.)

Carmen, Scene II. The curtain opens on the Tavern

Carmen, Scene I. The fight outside the cigarette factory. Carmen (JEANMAIRE) struggles with her fellow worker (JANE SHELDON)

Don José dances in the tavern of Lilas Pastia

The violent Carmen as we meet her in Scene I outside the cigarette factory

Carmen in the bedroom scene, Don José is watching her completely in her power

Don José draws the curtain.   Carmen, Scene III

Don José and Carmen.   The awakening, Scene III

Carmen provokes Don José.   Scene III

The pas de deux, Scene III.   Don José is completely in Carmen's power after having
shown the jealousy of the weak man

205

Carmen, Scene III. Don José watches Carmen

Carmen, Scene III.   The bedroom pas de deux ; the climax

Carmen arms Don José, Scene IV

Carmen, Scene IV

Clavé's scenery and costumes, as successful as Picasso's in *The Three Cornered Hat*, in translating the atmosphere of Spain play a major role in this ballet, especially in the fourth scene where there is little dancing and everything depends on conveying the atmosphere of Don José's abandonment. The moment the curtain rises on this forest of swinging wheels the drama is carried a stage further.

Clasping Don José, Carmen gives a final spasmodic twitch of her legs in the most realistic death scene in all ballet.

Carmen, Scene V. The death struggle to the beat of drums in which Roland Petit parallels the emotions of the final act of the *corrida* that is taking place inside the arena. Carmen is first provocative, contemptuous of his violence and sure that she can win him back. Then she is terrified as she realises that there is no escape. The drums continue to beat throughout the death scene—she trembles in her last agonies and then falls limply, mouth opening in a terrifyingly realistic manner — the drumming ceases — there is a long hushed pause—then very quietly the trilling theme melody of Carmen starts again as if to say that life must still go on. This is one of the most dramatic moments in all Ballet— where the use of the music emphasising the tragedy plays a great part.

Carmen, Scene V. 'The Moment of Truth.' The Bull lies dead in the Arena,
Carmen outside.

EPILOGUE
The Dancer's Physique

The dancer is an instrumentalist and the instrument is the dancer's body. Physical beauty therefore plays a major role in the dance as Gautier so repeatedly stressed. It is years of training that makes this natural beauty into an organised beauty that is consciously used.

Sentimentalists babble of the beauty of children dancing to the gramophone, delightfully unconscious of the effect they are creating. Sentimentalists also talk of child art and its message, confusing play and art which are but distantly related. Would those who delight in such naturalism and deplore the artificialities of ballet technique

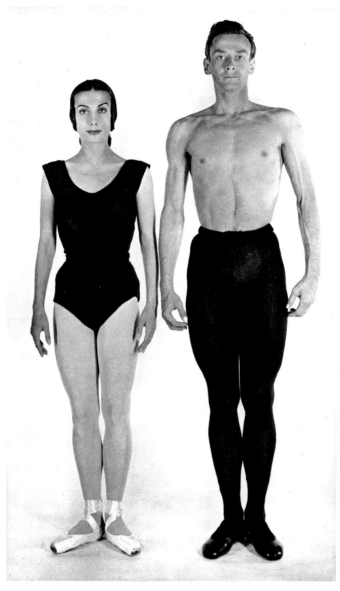

pay hard cash for their [s]eat Covent Garden or [at the] Metropolitan? I doub[t it]

Tamara Toumanova [and] George Skibine, depi[cted] here, are by nature mag[nifi]cent physical specim[ens] but it is their training [that] has given them the me[ans] of expressing themse[lves] through the dance.

Though thousands to[il to] learn ballet, improving t[heir] health, poise and co-o[rdi]nation, it is an art for [the] very few, those born [with] the perfect instrument [and] with the vocation to sp[end] a life time of work in w[hich] they are always pupil[s of] their maître de ballet h[ow]ever much glamour [they] may have for their pu[blic] the balletomanes.

TAMARA TOUMANOVA AND GEORGE SKIBINE

Arnold Haskell has written cogently on the importance of the physical attributes of the dancer and ballerina, writes Baron. Without these it is very difficult to reach perfection.

From a photographer's viewpoint, it is highly important. Toumanova and Skibine would appear to have the anatomical qualifications ideally suited to ballet dancing. In height, a ballerina should not exceed 5 ft. 5 in. or be less than 5 ft. 2 in. For a male dancer 5 ft. 9 in. would be tall enough and 5 ft. 6 in. the minimum. Only exceptional quality can overcome these limitations in height. Examine these pictures, which have been taken solely to reveal the anatomy—narrow waist, muscles which are smooth and pliable, small head set perfectly on the shoulders, legs which are long, absolutely straight and tapering, calves which touch each other when the legs are together, feet that are small and well shaped, small high buttocks, smooth diaphragm; carriage that is erect but lithe and supple; arms which are graceful, not over-muscled—and, particularly with the ballerina, shapely, graceful, lissom fingers.

Is there any other profession, or even game, which requires such a high degree of physical perfection to attain the ideal results?

TAMARA TOUMANOVA

TAMARA TOUMANOVA

GEORGE SKIBINE

MARGOT FONTEYN AND ROLAND PETIT

INDEX

All Ballets are listed under this heading. All Photographs are referred to in bold type.

Riabouchinska, Tania, 16, 51 ; in *Paganini*, 58, 169 ; in *Graduation Ball*, 167, **168**, **173-4** ; in *Les Présages, Scuola di Ballo, Jeux d'Enfants, Les Sylphides*, 169 ; in *Le Coq d'Or*, **192**

Rieti, 137

Robbins, Jerome, 19, 125 ; in *Fancy Free*, **126**, 127

Rodin, Auguste, 52

Rodolphe, Teddy, in *Les Forains*, **155-6**

Rostoff, Dimitri, in *Paganini*, 59

Rouault, 52, 53

Roy, Pierre, 21, 154

Sadovska, Helène, in *La Sylphide*, **161** ; in *Les Amours de Jupiter*, **162**

St. George, 25

Sauguet, 21, 155

Schoenberg, 132

Schooling, Elizabeth, in *Bar aux Folies Bergère*, **164**

Schwarz, Solange, in *Les Forains*, **155-6**

Shabalevsky, 146

Shearer, Moira, 22 ; in *Symphonic Variations*, **68**, **69** ; in *Les Sylphides*, **89** ; in *Cinderella*, **88**, **90**, **92-4** ; in *Les Patineurs*, **91**

Sheldon, in *Carmen*, **198**

Sibelius, 105

Sitwell, Sacheverell, 7-8

Skibine, George, 193, **212**, **215** ; in *Sebastian*, 190 ; in *Concerto Barocco*, **192**

Skorik, 22

Skouratoff, Vladimir, 22, 145, 186

Slavenska, Mia, in *Gaieté Parisienne*, **61**

Smith, Oliver, 127, 137, 190

Sokolova, Lydia, in *The Three Cornered Hat*, 65

Somes, Michael, 117 ; in *The Three Cornered Hat*, 65 ; in *Symphonic Variations*, **68**, **69**, **119**, **120**

Sovey, Raymond, 136

Spessivtseva, Olga, 16, 64, 158; in *Giselle*, 26

Staff, Frank, 163

Stravinsky, Igor, 20, 99, 154

Taglioni, 158

Tallchief, Marjorie, in *Giselle*, 26, **191**, **194** ; in *Concerto Barocco*, 191, **192**

Tchaikovsky, 21, 56, 88, 111, 112

Tchelitcheff, 21

Tcherina, Ludmilla, 145 ; in *Mephisto Valse*, **147**

Tchernicheva, Lubov, 15, 51 ; in *Francesca da Rimini*, 56 ; in *The Three Cornered Hat*, 65

Toumanova, Tamara, 16, 51, **176**, **177**, **212**, **213-14**; in *Giselle*, 26, **34-5** ; in *The Three Cornered Hat*, 65 ; in *Swan Lake*, **175**

Trefilova, 84

Tudor, Anthony, 19, 125, 137, 139, 142, 163 ; in *Pillar of Fire*, 132 ; in *Jardin aux Lilas*, **136** ; in *Waltz Academy*, **138**

Turner, Harold, 163 ; in *The Three Cornered Hat*, 65, 113 ; in *Spectre de la Rose* and *La Boutique Fantasque*, 113; in *Job*, **114-15**

Valéry, Paul, 149

Vaslavina, Norman, in *Waltz Academy*, 138

Vaudoyer, 41

Verchinina, Nina, 51, 54

Verlaine, Paul, 151

Vladimir, Grand Duke, 14

Vyroubova, Nina, 17, 18, 22 ; in *Giselle*, 26 ; in *La Sylphide*, **158-61**

Wakhevitch, 21, 42, 151

Woizikovski, Leon, 51, 146 ; in *The Three Cornered Hat*, 65

Youskevitch, Igor, in *Giselle*, **34-5**, **38**